Best Pub Walks in Derbyshire

Martin Smith

Published by Sigma Leisure – an imprint of
Sigma Press, 1 South Oak Lane, Wilmslow, Cheshire SK9 6AR, England.

British Library Cataloguing in Publication Data
A CIP record for this book is available from the British Library.

ISBN: 1-85058-337-4

Typesetting and Design by: Sigma Press, Wilmslow, Cheshire.

Maps by: Martin Smith

Text photographs: Martin Smith

Cover photograph: Shoulder of Mutton, Osmaston; Chris Rushton

Printed by: Manchester Free Press

General Disclaimer

Whilst every effort has been made to ensure that the information given in this book is correct, neither the publisher nor the author accept any responsibility for any inaccuracy.

CONTENTS

INTRODUCTION

THE WALKS

KEY TO MAPS:

Road used for walk

Track used for walk }

Obvious footpath used for walk }

Intermittent footpath used for walk

No obvious path, but route of walk

Other road

Other track }

Other obvious footpath }

Other intermittent footpath

Railway

River, arrow shows direction of flow

Church/Chapel

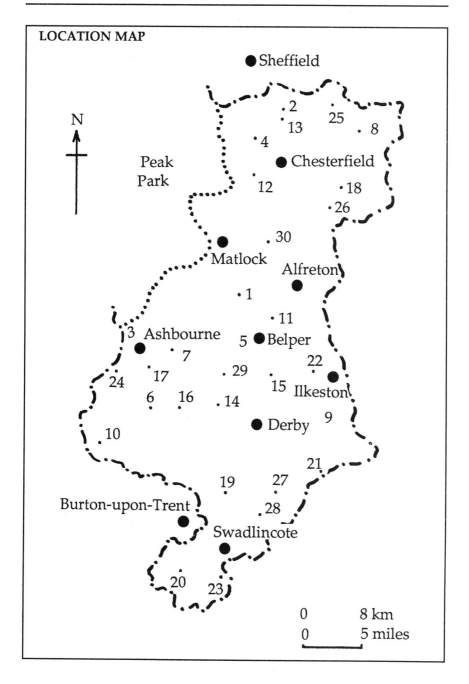

LOCATION MAP

DERBYSHIRE:
ONLY THE SEA IS MISSING

It has been said that the only feature Derbyshire lacks to make it scenically complete, is a coastline. Nevertheless, it is still one of the most beautiful counties in England. To the north are the high moors of the Peak District. In the centre there are the limestone dales and hills. To the south lie the broad swathes of the Vale of Trent. Along the eastern side of the county is the coalfield belt, but don't let that put you off. The industry that shows up graphically on the old One Inch to the Mile maps, has largely gone, taking thousands of jobs with it and altering whole communities. However, the disfigurement that the mines and their attendant heavy industries wrought, has been ably replaced by the various local authorities, with a large measure of assistance from Nature. Where once there was soot and grime there are now fields, wild flowers and delightful walks.

About this book . . .

This book concentrates on that part of Derbyshire outside the Peak District. Anyone wanting similar walks in the Peak should obtain the two Peak District Pub Walks books, also published by Sigma Press. This book covers an area extending from the boundary of Sheffield in the north, right down the eastern edge of Derbyshire to Ripley and Belper. It then takes in a great tract of countryside southwards to the Trent and Dove. Finally there are walks in that forgotten part of the county, south of the Trent, in Calke Park and on the Staffordshire, Leicestershire borders.

Of paths and designer gear

For the most part, the paths covered in this book fall into two distinct groups. Those on the populous eastern side are largely well used and maintained. Those in the deeply rural area around Ashbourne, see little use or maintenance. Navigation here needs both the patience and faith of a saint. Maintenance and signing of paths are largely the responsibility of the County Council, though some District, Parish and Town councils have arrangements to maintain paths in their areas. Similarly some voluntary groups have adopted paths to keep them open and in good repair. Any problems should first be addressed to the County or District Council.

There is also a contrast in the users of the paths in these two areas. The eastern paths are used more by locals for dog walking or strolling, or even going to work or shopping. Designer boots, breeches and waterproofs look singularly out of place here. Even a rucksack is greeted with a raised eyebrow. The southern, rural paths, see little local use, so the only walkers you are likely to see are discerning people like yourself, refugees from the National Park "motorways". Again, designer gear is likely to be the source of a wry smile. But carry a well-thumbed OS Pathfinder Map and wear a pair of well-worn boots and this will quickly lead to a chat about the conflicts between farmers and walkers, or other staples like the weather, beer and the ruination of footpaths because of "too many guide books". At this point, hide your book and suddenly remember your appointment at the local hostelry.

A Welcome at the Village Inn

One of the great bonuses of going for a walk, is the ability to visit a range of local hostelries for a pint of ale or whatever beverage takes your fancy, either at lunchtime or at the end of the walk. The village inn has for centuries welcomed travellers, whether they arrived on foot or by some other means. Many country pubs now derive their livelihood from leisure drinkers, visitors to the countryside from the nearby towns, than from a tiny local clientele. However, there is a stark contrast between the villages in the more populated eastern part of the county, where some villages have three or four pubs and those in the very rural south and west where the village local seems to be just clinging to life.

However, in either case the tradition of hospitality and "keeping a good pint" remains the same. For the latter, some credit must go to the Campaign for Real Ale, better known as CAMRA, who have fought to keep the real British beers on tap in pubs and inns throughout the country. Credit to the brewers themselves, who realised, in the nick of time, that they were in danger of losing a wonderful traditional drink. All the pubs in this book sell at least one "real" ale and many have guest beers as well for true devotees.

About the Pubs

The landlords of the pubs mentioned in this book have all been consulted and asked if they welcome ramblers. They do, but this is not the Peak, where ramblers are a sizeable proportion of the clientele. For the most part ramblers in these pubs will be a rare breed.

I have tried to give accurate information about beers sold, times of opening etc. Like everything else in life, these things change. Recent legislation regarding brewery ownership of pubs means that the beers sold may change more rapidly than might have been anticipated.

Most pubs now serve food and this is indicated in the text. This is part of an alteration in the trading pattern of the rural inn, many having to sell food to survive. It is an important source of income to the landlord. You are therefore not likely to endear yourself to the publican if you get out your own sandwiches and start to eat them in the lounge bar! Unless stated, you should presume that you are not allowed to eat your own food on the premises. However, this usually doesn't apply to food eaten outside the pub.

Similarly there is the situation of your muddy boots. You would not expect a visitor to walk across your lounge carpet in size 10 boots covered in cow muck, so why should you do it in a pub? Many pubs are now carpeted, even in the public bar and signs saying, "No muddy boots" are commonplace in regular walking areas. In this area, where walkers are not great in number, such signs may not appear, but use your common sense and either take your boots off, or cover them with clean overshoes – nothing technical, a plastic carrier bag is perfectly effective and cheap.

Every landlord included in this book is happy to welcome families, though you are likely to be confined to an area away from the bar. This is the law, not a whim of the landlord. Usually, there are gardens or other outdoor seating, which in many respects are better for families anyhow, at least in summer. If you are in doubt, pop your head round the door and ask if it's OK to bring the family in.

Despite the move to serving food, the pubs listed in this book are still primarily village inns, not restaurants serving beer. As such they follow the old philosophy of the rural hostelry, welcoming the thirsty traveller, especially if they have done something so unusual as to arrive on foot!

Don't Drink and Drive

There is an obvious snag to extolling the virtues of ale in this car-dominated society. It cannot be stressed too highly that alcohol and driving are a lethal combination, if not for the driver, then potentially for some other poor innocent. If you have to get to these walks by car, let someone else do the driving for you if you want to sample the beers. Better still, use the bus or train and help boost the local economy even more.

Public Transport

Rural bus and train travel is an interesting experience in its own right and can be as much fun as the walk or the session in the local pub. All the walks in this book can be accessed by public transport, though it has to be said that occasionally the service provided is sparse in the extreme. If you are using the bus or train you should always check times in advance. Derbyshire County Council produce an excellent series of timetable books detailing all services in the county. The County Council also runs a BUSLINE telephone service for would-be travellers. At the time of writing, the correct numbers are:

Derby (01332) 292200 or Chesterfield (01246) 250450.

Some rail information is also available from these numbers, but ring British Rail for more detailed information about times and fares.

About the Walks

There are 30 walks for you to choose from, varying from 3 to 8 miles. Obviously the amount of exertion required varies too. However, the area covered is not like the Peak District. There are no long steep ascents or miles of bog covered moor. For the most part, Derbyshire beyond the Peak is a tamed and gentle country for walkers, but as mentioned in other books in this series, there are a few golden rules to follow.

What you Need

While you don't need designer gear for these walks, a stout pair of boots or walking shoes is essential. Even in the populous east, it is best to go prepared with a light rucksack, waterproofs, a spare jumper and a snack.

Most other people you meet will be out for an afternoon stroll a few hundred yards from their front door. Arguably they don't need such equipment, but you do. There's nothing worse than travelling home in wet clothes. Derbyshire's weather can be notoriously fickle. Beware the comment from a passing local, "It's black o'er our Billy's". This will undoubtedly mean there's rain on the way, though who Billy is and where he lives is anyone's guess.

It's always a good idea to let someone know where you are going. This is not to say that you should display a notice on your car. That would be asking for trouble, but a word with your neighbour or a friend would be no bad thing. Although you're not going mountaineering, some of these walks are on paths that see very little use and are surprisingly remote. An accident here and you'd not be found for days.

Maps

The walks should be easy to follow using the instructions and maps in the book. However, for each walk the appropriate OS Pathfinder map (1:25000 scale), is indicated. These maps show every field boundary, right of way, track and stream. They also show a wealth of additional detail, which cannot be included in a book of this nature. I strongly recommend that you invest in some of these maps. However, I do acknowledge that, to buy the number required to cover all the walks is a daunting prospect, unless you are intending to do some exploration of your own in the same area. Many public libraries have a map lending service, so this possibility should be examined. Alternatively the OS 1:50000 sheets cover a much larger area and while they lack the detail, they do at least show the paths. Don't just rely on the maps in the book. With the best will in the world, you could take a wrong turning and be completely lost without a wider ranging map.

The Countryside

You must remember that the countryside is not just a playground for you. It is a working environment. Respect it, respect those who work in it and those who live in it. Make sure you leave it no worse for your visit.

Derbyshire: a potted history

The history of settlement and therefore footpaths, goes back some 7000 years. The areas used by these early settlers were the uplands for the most part, or at least the well drained areas. There were significant concentrations of population in the limestone areas and on the high gritstone moors of the Peak, but there are important archeological sites outside this area, most obviously at Cresswell Crags and Swarkestone.

During the Iron Age, life seems to have been more subjected to strife, leading to the construction of hillforts and other defensive works. The fort at Markland Grips, near Clowne, is a good example.

The Roman occupation created more signs of settlement in the lowlands than in the uplands. The east and south of the county was traversed by a network of roads, of which Ryknield Street is the best known. In this book, various Roman routes will be encountered and one, Longwalls Lane near Belper, forms a major part of the particular walk.

The withdrawal of the Roman legions eventually led to the Saxon occupation of most of Derbyshire. By the 7th century the kingdom of Mercia had been established, with its capital at Repton and a thriving little settlement at Northworthy (Derby), close to the Roman fort at Little Chester.

Christianity, which came to the area in late Roman times, may well have survived the initial paganism of the Saxons. Place name evidence, like the use of the word "eccles" (from the Latin "ecclesia" and akin to the Welsh "eglwys", both meaning "church"), seems to suggest this may be the case. Certainly by the 7th century there were well established churches at Repton and Wirksworth.

The Danish invasion of the 9th century saw control of Derbyshire pass to these new arrivals. England was divided and Derbyshire became part of the Danelaw. Their main town in the area was Derby, the old North-worthy being abandoned. Inevitable assimilation followed and by 1066 England was one country again, just in time for a new Norseman, or Norman, invasion. Domesday Book gives a graphic record of Derbyshire at this time and most of the settlements existing today were in existence then in some form. The network of tracks and paths which formed the routes between these settlements is the basis of our road and path system today, though their function has changed from a utilitarian one to that of leisure.

The Norman and medieval period saw the widespread construction of stone churches and castles. While the latter are ruinous or vanished completely, Derbyshire possesses a wealth of beautiful churches, scattered round the county. The Normans also brought with them a system of farming which has left a significant imprint on the lower lands of the county in particular. The great open fields, divided and worked in strips until enclosed in the 18th and 19th centuries, can still be traced in many places.

Agricultural change and indeed rural disasters like plague, wiped out whole villages. The maps of southern and western Derbyshire have many references to "Site of Medieval Village", some of which are visited on these walks. Ruins of any kind are evocative, but these tumbled, grass covered mounds are more compelling than most. Whole communities lived and worked here and have vanished almost as if they had never been. The medieval period, until the end of the Wars of the Roses must have been troubled times. However, in the stability which followed, the Derbyshire gentry built themselves some fine houses, ranging from the near palaces like Hardwick, to the more modest Halls and Manors which grace many a village. The Tudor dissolution of the monasteries and abbeys saw the local gentry taking advantage of opportunities to acquire land and build houses. Derbyshire is sadly lacking in monastic remains, but in the glorious chancel arch of Dale Abbey we possess a poignant reminder of pre-Reformation England.

The Civil War had its impact on Derbyshire as on other areas of the kingdom. Families and communities were divided and roving bands of soldiery, from either side, did great damage to life, economy and property. Some destruction from this war still survives in the county and a number of the walks have Civil War tales attached to them.

The two centuries that followed the Civil War, saw Derbyshire change dramatically, with agricultural and then industrial developments, the latter particularly in the eastern part of the county. In this period of change, the march of Bonnie Prince Charlie's army in 1745 seems almost like a dream sequence, a throwback to earlier, more unsettled times. The '45 stopped at Swarkestone, so various pubs, towns and villages between there and Ashbourne have tales of the Highlanders. The army probably came down the well established drove routes and some of our walks will cross their path.

This economic change also produced dramatic developments on the transport front. The ancient routeways, scarcely changed from medieval times, were utterly inadequate and the great surge of turnpike road building followed, leaving the old routes to return to grass and peace. Many of these are our footpaths of today, while the turnpikes are our main roads.

The industrialisation of Derbyshire eventually produced a clear division between the rural west and the densely populated, industrial east. This is still evident today, though the industry has changed dramatically and where once iron foundries and coal-mines stood, there are now freshly landscaped areas.

Footnote

Field boundaries are removed or altered. Trees are cut down or new ones are planted. Buildings are demolished or constructed. This book was written as a result of research in 1992/3, so please accept my apologies in advance if you find the description no longer matches the facts. Hopefully the text is so worded that the route should be easy to follow despite the loss of a few landmarks. Nevertheless, I would be surprised if I don't feel my ears burning on occasion! My thanks to all those who have helped me in this project, in particular to my long suffering wife, who has been walked round more obscure footpaths and ventured into more well hidden hostelries than she ever thought possible.

Happy rambling and enjoy your pint.

1: ALDERWASLEY

The Route: Alderwasley Church – Alderwasley Park –Shining Cliff Woods – Johnson's Wire Works – Shining Cliff YHA – Typeclose Plantation – Ranch Farm – The Bear – Willetts Farm – Little Hayes Farm –Ridge Wood – Kennel Wood – Alderwasley

Distance: 4.5 miles (7.25 km). Allow 2 – 2.5 hours exclusive of pub stop

Start: Entrance to Alderwasley Park. Grid reference: 326531, limited roadside parking

Map(s): OS 1:25000 Pathfinder Series No.794, Crich

How to get there:

By Public Transport: School-days only service to Alderwasley. Daily train and bus service to Ambergate, picking up the walk at Johnson's Wire Works, an extra mile in each direction.

By Car: A6 to Whatstandwell. Junction on western side of bridge signed to Alderwasley. Then follow New Road and Higg Lane.

The Pub

The pub is The Olde Bear Inn, serving Bass Beers as well as Ivanhoe and Highgate Mild. There are tables and seats outside for walkers with sandwiches, but the pub serves meals at lunchtimes and evenings every day. Opening times are 11am – 3pm and 6pm – 11pm, Mondays to Fridays, 11am – 11pm, Saturdays and 12noon – 10.30pm on Sundays. Children are welcome at the pub and there is a children's play area outside, fenced off from the road. For the staying visitor, there's a bridal suite, or, if your aspirations are more modest, there's a caravan site alongside the pub.

The Walk

Before leaving the parking place, look over the wall for a very pleasant view over the ornamental ponds, to the church and the Georgian mansion of Alderwasley Hall. The church was built in 1850 in the grounds of the Hall. Alderwasley Hall was the home of the Hurt family

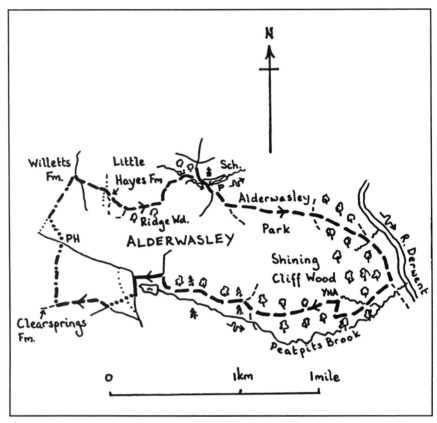

for many years, but is now a school. The view is quintessentially English; geese on the pond, the juxtaposition of great house and church and rooks in the trees around it. The old chapel, which contains some 16th century workmanship, lies up the road from the "new" church.

Go over the step stile by the gate and into the park. Follow the track up past the war memorial, with the school playing fields on the left. There is a good view across the Derwent valley to Crich Stand, while to your left is the frontage of Alderwasley Hall.

The path leaves the track to go left, round the corner of the playing field fence, heading for a metal gate across the parkland. The path is not obvious underfoot at this point, but it soon becomes clear as it joins another track. Keep heading for the metal gate, ignoring another track leading off left and downhill. Near the gate there is a little stone waymarker.

Minute Moles?

Do not go through the gate, but keep to the left of the fence on a terraced path, with wide views over the valley. There is a stone seat part way along this stretch, but it is early in the walk to be wanting a rest. The piles of stones in the parkland and on the right, are not prehistoric remains, but boulders bulldozed out of the way for agricultural "improvement". In early Spring this path has tiny piles of yellowish earth on it, only 3 –4cm across, with a hole in the centre. They are not caused by a minute species of mole, but by "digger" wasps, newly emerged from their cocoons.

Go over the stile ahead and continue through the parkland, past some very ancient trees, to another stile in the wall ahead. The approach to this stile is over a wet patch, by a broken trough.

Shining Cliff Woods

Go through the stile and enter Shining Cliff Woods, now in the owner-ship of the National Trust. Immediately inside the wood there are paths left, right and straight on. Your route lies straight ahead, on the right of way, descending through the woods into the Derwent valley.

This is a beautiful wood, a mixture of mainly deciduous trees, with a dense growth of bilberry etc. beneath. The only drawback is that the path doubles up as a stream bed and it is always wet!

Continue down through the wood, until another, wider path joins from the left, by a set of fire beaters. Bear right here, still tending downwards, ignoring narrow paths running off to the right. The noises of civilisation are now apparent in the form of the railway and the A6, but neither can be seen, though there is an occasional glimpse of the River Derwent through the trees on the left.

The broad track descends to a stile by a gate. This is the boundary of National Trust property. What a contrast it is, with a waste dump on the left and the Trust's wood on the right. Continue along the track, with various bits of derelict machinery on your left, until you almost reach the first buildings of Johnson's Wire Works. Here there is a broad track going off to the right and this is your route.

Public Transport Users Start Here!

(Public transport users will join the walk at this point, having come from

Ambergate and through the middle of the wire works. As you reach the
northern end of the works, there is a sign on a tree, pointing left and
indicating that this is the route to Shining Cliff Youth Hostel).

Follow this track up past the recent logging operations, ignoring other
paths to the right. Re-enter the wood and leave the industrial despoila-
tion behind. The track rises steadily through the trees, a mixture of
conifers and deciduous. Listen for the drumming of woodpeckers as you
climb up the valley of Peatpits Brook. A stream crosses the path, which
is muddy at this point. Shortly afterwards there is a junction of paths.

The Grith Pioneers

The direction sign proclaims that the route to the Youth Hostel is to the
right, but the more interesting sign is that of the Grith Pioneers, who
exhort you to look after this woodland. There is a map on this sign, but
it is too stylised to be of much use and it doesn't say where you are in
any case.

Turn right and head up to Shining Cliff Youth Hostel, which soon
appears ahead, nestled below the rocks. The main path turns sharp left
to the hostel by another Pioneers sign, which boasts the same map as the
previous example. Go left and up the track, passing the hostel on your
right and the cycle shed on the left. Shining Cliff itself is the craggy
outcrop behind the hostel and alongside the path. Continue up the path,
passing another wooden hut on the left. Then follow the wide track
through the delightful mixed woodland. Where the path forks, just
beyond the brick built water tank, keep right. There are odd clearings in
the wood to the sides of the path, with piles or rings of stones in them.
Quite what purpose they serve is not clear.

The path is now almost level and shortly crosses the remains of a stone
wall. A little way further on, but still in the wood, there is a metal post
in the middle of the path, heralding the boundary of Pioneer territory. A
third Pioneer sign, with its ubiquitous map, is reached at a triangular
junction of paths. Bear right here, and continue for a short way with a
fence on your left.

A Muddy Traverse of Typeclose Plantation

The path forks again and there is a stile on the left, though it is not
needed as there is a wide gap in the fence. Go left here into Typeclose
Plantation, which is mainly conifers.

The path is level and distinct. It is also muddy and churned up by horses, though it isn't a bridleway according to the map. There are a number of very wet patches where the pedestrian route dives off through the trees to avoid the worst of the mud. At one particular quagmire, passage is eased by a few conveniently placed stones on the right.

In the midst of the gloom of the spruce trees, the path bears right, crosses a stream in an obviously artificial course, then runs alongside a fence on the left. There is the glimpse of a pond through the trees to the left, then the path reaches a stile. Go straight on, through another stile and thus reach the road.

Nocturnal Map Reading Made Easy

At the road go left and walk down the lane to its junction with Belper Lane. Unusually for such a rural location, there is a street light here, suspended on a wire between two poles. At least if you do this walk at midnight you'll be able to read the map!

Go left at the junction, passing the farm with its neatly-tended verge, to reach a footpath sign on the right. Pass through the stile and into the field. The path is not obvious here, but the way ahead lies towards the prominent frame of a building seen to the left. The exit stile is part way along the left-hand wall of the field.

In the next field, the path continues on the same alignment towards the building. The pub is also in view, to the right, a large white building. Disconcertingly, you seem to be heading away from it at this stage. Another stile is negotiated and the path, still heading for the frame building, crosses a final field to a stile out onto the road.

By Stage Coach to Ranch Farm

Turn right here and go down the track to Ranch Farm with its stage coach sign. Negotiate the cattle-grid and pass the dog-guarded modern bungalow. There is a quick glimpse to the right to Crich Stand, then continue along the track towards Clear Springs Farm.

The forest of radio masts on the skyline to the left of the farm marks Alport Heights. However, at the white gate, well before the farm, there is a stile on the right. Go over this stile. The pub is now ahead, but the path is not quite as straight forward as it might appear.

Keep the wall on the left as you walk down to the stile by the gate at the far end of the field. Negotiate the stile and, keeping a weather eye on the horses which regularly graze this field, head towards a little gate on the opposite side of the field. The gate is just to the left of a corrugated metal trough structure.

The Olde Bear at Alderwasley

Go through the gate and over the metal bridge across the stream to another stile. A final dash alongside the wall takes you to a further stile that deposits you on the road right opposite the pub.

The Olde Bear

On leaving the pub, make your way through their car park to a well hidden stile in the far wall, just alongside a floodlight pole. This stile takes you into fields again, but the path is not obvious underfoot. Head across the field to the right of the buildings, towards the twin electricity poles. In the field corner there is a double stile, which requires some agility to negotiate. Its purpose is to keep sheep and lambs in, so please respect it. On the far side of the second stile there is quite a drop down into the field, but there is a good view over Alderwasley and to Crich.

In this next field, head for the twin poles again. On reaching the wall, go right and proceed down the field keeping the wall/fence on your left. Ignore the green lane leading off left and continue down, by a hedge now, to a stile by the gateway to Willetts Farm. Go over this stile and past the railway van body to another stile. This exits onto the road in the midst of a cluster of very attractive farm buildings and cottages. In particular look out for the spring and well, just on your right as you reach the road.

Go right, along the road for a short distance, passing some immaculate cottage gardens. At the footpath sign by the electricity pole, go left, through a gate into fields again.

Not Such a Little House

The path runs alongside a wall on the left, skirts a clump of holly trees and goes through a gateway into another field. Still keeping the wall on the left, go through this field to another stile into the lane opposite Little House. This is part of the complex of buildings shown on the map as Little Hayes Farm. Go right here, along the lane, which wriggles its way between the buildings before emerging into the open, with a good view towards Crich.

Where the lane goes sharply right, before the green and white caravan, there is a path to the left, through a stile. This goes into a patch of woodland, the remnant of Ridge Wood. As the name suggests, this wood sits, or sat, on the ridge between Pendleton Brook and Peatpits Brook. Much of the wood has been cleared however, and the cattle graze in what's left, so there will be no natural regeneration.

The path keeps to the lower boundary of the "wood", with the wall on the left and a pleasant view over Alderwasley. Two stiles are negotiated, followed by two more in quick succession, as the path drops onto the driveway to the left of Ridgewood Cottage.

In the Dog House?

Go left here, down the driveway, and follow it down through the gateway towards the white house. The track goes left, then right to skirt the white house, known as The Kennels. It then crosses Pendleton Brook in Kennel Wood, turns right and eventually emerges on the road almost opposite the entrance to Alderwasley School and Church. Go right to reach the starting point and your car.

2: APPERKNOWLE

The Route: Apperknowle – The Blackamoor – Troway – Fold Farm – Marsh Lane – West Handley – Butchersick Farm – Apperknowle

Distance: 4.4 miles (7km)

Start: Yellow Lion, Apperknowle, Grid reference: 384783

Map(s): OS 1:25000 Pathfinder Series No. 761 Chesterfield & 762 Worksop South

How to get there:

By Public Transport: There is a Monday to Saturday bus service from Chesterfield and a daily service from Sheffield and Eckington.

By Car: Follow the B6057 from Dronfield or Whittington, then take the minor road signed to Apperknowle when you get to Unstone. Whether you come from north or south it is just after a railway bridge. Go up the hill to the T-junction at the top and turn left. There is plenty of roadside parking opposite the Yellow Lion.

The Pub

The pub is the Gate Inn at Troway. The decor has a footballing theme, but it is a surprisingly rural pub given its proximity to Sheffield. There are two bars and walkers are welcome in either, but you are requested to remove muddy boots. Normal opening hours are kept, but no food is served, except crisps etc. Burtonwood Beers are available on draught and the Traditional Bitter is particularly palatable. There's a beer garden outside, but for that chilly mid winter walk there are also welcoming real fires in the bars.

The Walk

From the Yellow Lion, walk down the road towards the Reference Point pub. This pub closed while the book was being written. It used to be the Travellers Rest and owned by the late lamented Scarsdale Brewery. The unusual name of Reference Point perpetuates an old pub tradition of naming inns after race horses.

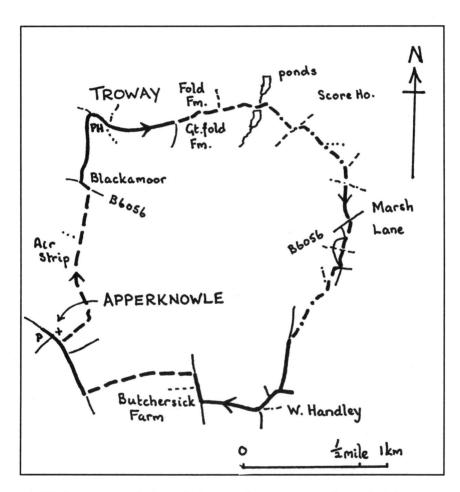

A Trip Round Appleknowle International Airport

Just past the Methodist chapel, go left at the road junction sign, into a narrow lane, half choked with nettles. This quickly rises away from the road, giving a good view back over Unstone, towards the high moors of the Peak District. The lane turns sharp left to run northwards towards Sheffield. This route is a bridleway and it clearly sees some use by horses as there are places where it is quite badly churned up and muddy. None of these are impassable however. Soon you catch sight of a wind sock and then the lane runs across the end of a little air strip. Be ready to duck. This is the summit of the lane and now Sheffield can be seen ahead, with the water tower at Norton a prominent feature. If distant views to cities are not to your liking, there is a pleasant rural view to the right, down into the Moss Valley.

The lane soon reaches the B6056 and here you turn left, along the road. At the Blackamoor, a Stones house, turn right along the road signed to Troway. The lane is lightly used and soon begins to descend quite steeply, with glimpses ahead across the valley to the Sheffield suburbs. For all that you are very close to the outskirts of the city, this area has a surprisingly deep rural feel about it. Take care at the bend by The Grange as the visibility is not good.

A Well Hung Gate

Still descending, you now reach The Gate Inn at Troway. This lovely little pub sells Burtonwood beers and has a pleasant little beer garden. Note the amusing inn sign, "This gate hangs well and hinders none. Refresh and pay and travel on". Who could resist such blandishments? When you eventually leave The Gate and Troway behind, carry on along the lane past Doe Lea Farm, with good views down into the valley on your left. At the Memorial seat the road turns sharp right, but you continue ahead down the "Private" road, which despite the sign is a public footpath. The farm lane passes between Fold Farm and Greenfold Farm and where the track splits four ways, go down the narrow, tree lined route straight ahead. This soon reaches another fork, where there are two stiles. Yours is the right hand, waymarked one, which takes you into open fields. The path runs down by the side of a sloe hedge to reach a gate and stile in the bottom left-hand corner. Again this is waymarked and the path continues down the left-hand side of the field to reach the mill ponds in the bottom.

A waymarked stile leads onto the dam between the ponds. Like most such stretches of water near urban areas, this is heavily frequented by anglers, so keep a sharp look out for flying hooks. The path crosses the overflow weir on a bridge, then rises away to the left through the trees, waymarked in places, to reach a stile. This deposits you in open fields again and a waymark shows that the path runs straight up the middle of the field, keeping to the right of the solitary bush. In this manner you will arrive at a post and gateway, leading out onto a narrow, rough track. Here map number 761 deserts you and you need 762.

Go left here, briefly, then right at a stile and so back into fields again. Bear left across the field to reach a stile in the hedge about 50 metres up from the corner. Now continue right, alongside the hedge, eventually arriving at a stile by a gate. Cross the chatter track and go up through the gorse to reach a stile in the top hedge, just to the left of the gate. Go right here, along the track into Marsh Lane.

Chips for Dinner, Tea and Supper

The track soon becomes a proper road called School Lane. The school is on the left, as is the village pump. At the junction with the main road, go straight on, down the narrow path to the left of the chip shop. This comes out onto a road again in a housing estate. Follow the road until it bends to the left, where there is a junction. Here go right, up a path by a chain link fence to the children's playing field. The path now runs along the backs of the gardens, and is in regular use, if only for doggy walking; take care! Just before the last houses, the path veers away to the right to a stile. An extensive view now opens up to the left. Carry straight on from the stile, under the wires of the electricity line, towards the solitary tree on the opposite side of the field. A gap in the right-hand hedge, to the right of the pylon takes you out onto the road.

Smoke and Steam

On reaching the road, go left, noting that you are back on map 761 again. Walk down the road, with a fine view ahead over Chesterfield, until you reach a T-junction. Here you turn right and then at the next junction, veer left, following the sign to West Handley. At the junction just before the 30 mph sign, go right, past Ash Lane Farm, which is partly thatched. Continue along this quiet lane, passing the pond on the right, which looks as if it is on the site of a small quarry. There is an extensive view to the left along this lane, with the billows of smoke and steam from the distant carbonisation plant at Wingerworth all too prominent. At the T-junction, turn right along Long Lane for a couple of hundred metres. Just past Butchersick Farm, there is a signpost on the left-hand side of the road indicating a footpath. Leave the road at this point and enter fields. The path runs along the right-hand hedge, crossing a wet patch on a bridge of old railway sleepers, then running up past the farm to a gateway at the top of the field. In the next field, keep the wall on your left and you'll not go far wrong, despite admiring the view ahead, which takes in the eastern fringing hills of the Peak District. Don't let you eyes wander too much, or you'll come up hard against the next stile. Negotiate this and proceed down the right-hand side of the field, by the wall, to reach a gap by a post. Tumble through the gap onto the road and go right. The Reference Point is about three hundred metres ahead and Apperknowle village and your car about 200 metres beyond that.

The Gate Inn, Troway

3: ASHBOURNE

The Route: Ashbourne (Mappleton Lane Car Park) – Callow Top –Mappleton – Okeover Bridge – Thorpe Church – Spend Lane Farm – Callow Top Farm – Tissington Trail – Ashbourne (MLCP)

Distance: 5 miles (8.25km)

Start: Mappleton Lane Car Park on the Tissington Trail, Grid reference: 176469

Map(s): OS 1:25000 Pathfinder Series No. 810 Ashbourne and Churnet Valley

How to get there:

By Public Transport: Daily services to Ashbourne from Derby and Manchester. Infrequent services from Buxton and Matlock. The infrequent local bus service from Ashbourne to Ilam runs past the car park, but the start of the walk is only half a mile from the bus station in any case.

By Car: From Ashbourne Market Square, (A515), turn left and follow the signs to Mappleton and the car park.

The Pub

The Okeover Arms at Mappleton sits comfortably alongside the unusual little church. A veritable thirst after righteousness. The pub serves Burton Ales and provides food at lunchtimes and evenings. Opening hours are 11am – 3pm Monday to Saturday, 12noon – 3pm and 7pm – 10.30pm on Sundays. Families are welcomed and there is an outdoor seating area. Hikers are also welcomed but are asked to remove muddy boots. There is a collection of photos in the bar spanning the years from the mid 1800s to the early part of this century.

The Walk

Leave the car park along the Tissington Trail, passing the cycle hire centre on the right. The Trail was formerly the Buxton Ashbourne railway line, closed to passengers even before Dr. Beeching was heard of.

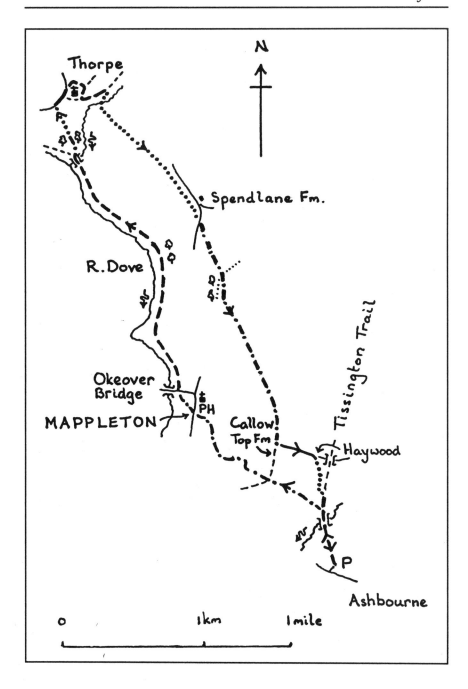

It was subsequently purchased by the Peak National Park and converted into a walking and cycling route. The Trail initially runs on an embankment, but soon dips sharply to a bridge over the Bentley Brook. Students of railways will be surprised at the steepness of the gradient on either side of the bridge, but this is because the seven arch viaduct which previously spanned the valley was demolished and the new bridge and approaches substituted.

Once you have climbed away from the new bridge and reached the top of the embankment again, you pass through a gateway. Now look out for a path leading off to the left, down a flight of steps, to a stile in the fence. This takes you into a steeply sloping field. The exit stile is in the top right-hand corner, though it's not obvious from the point you enter the field, nor is the path to it very distinct.From the top of the field the spire of Ashbourne church can be seen to the left.

Continue ahead in the next field, keeping the hedge to your left, but bearing gently away from it to reach a gate and stile between two ash trees. The wind-blasted trees on Minninglow can be seen on the northern horizon. The path now keeps close to the right-hand hedge to reach a stile. Ignore the gateway to the right, which leads to Callow Top Farm and carry straight on, still alongside the right-hand hedge to reach another stile. Here a view opens up, taking in Lower Dovedale. Okeover Hall can be seen on the far side of the river, while to the right is Thorpe Cloud and Thorpe village. Continue ahead, descending now towards the Dove valley, heading just to the right of Okeover Hall and thus reach a stile. Follow the fence cum hedge on your right and go down more steeply to reach a gap by the holly tree. Pass through the gap and onto a very wet patch, now following the right-hand hedge across the slope of the hill. Mappleton village and the pub are now in sight. The path is now obvious on the ground, though narrow as it descends through a few more fields, with the houses of Mappleton coming ever closer on your left. The view up the Dove towards Thorpe Cloud, is very fine, but don't let this distract you, or you'll miss the stile on the left, just before the pub. This stile takes you onto a confined path which soon deposits you on the road, in the middle of Mappleton village and very close to the inn.

Mappleton

Mappleton, or Mapleton as it is sometimes spelt, is a lovely little village alongside the River Dove. It was formerly in the ownership of the Okeover family of Okeover Hall on the Staffordshire bank, hence the name of the pub. It is a brick built village, totally different from the nearby Peak District limestone villages. The church is most unusual, with its pillared porch. It was built in the 18th century, replacing a 15th century structure of which there is now no trace. It is known locally as Little St. Pauls because of its domed roof. Also in the village are some fine almshouses, dating back to 1727, and an ancient manor house. Nearby is the mock Elizabethan Callow Hall, which was actually built in the 1850s.

"Little St Paul's"

The Okeover Arms

On leaving the Okeover Arms, go across the road and through the stile in the wall opposite, following the sign to Dovedale. The path bears right, across the field, heading for the lovely arched bridge. There is a stile in the wall, just before the bridge. The bridge spans the River Dove, which here is the county boundary. Over the bridge lies Staffordshire, but this walk stays firmly on the Derbyshire side. Cross the road with care as the visibility for drivers coming from Staffordshire is not good because of the humped backed nature of the bridge. A stile in the wall gives access to the riverside path.

Into The National Park

At first the path keeps close to the river bank, but after a couple of fields the route bears right to cut off a loop of the river. The river bank is rejoined at a gap in the hedge and the next field is decidedly wet and muddy. It would not take too much rain to make the river flood at this point, so pick your days with care. A footbridge leads over a tributary stream into an area of scrubby woodland. You are now in the Peak National Park. Still keep close to the river's edge through a series of stiles, with Thorpe Cloud in view ahead, until you reach the stile alongside the horse jump. Thorpe Cloud is the limestone hill at the entrance to Dovedale. It is now in the ownership of the National Trust. The next field is crossed still alongside the river, to reach a further stile by a gate. This leads into an area of woodland and the path crosses a stream on a bridge wide enough to take a tractor.

Immediately over the stream, go right, leaving the riverside path, to ascend a narrow trail up by the stream. The steepening ground and the closeness of the trees and bushes, forces the path away from the stream. Another path crosses, but keep straight on and up, until you reach what appears to be an impenetrable area of blackthorn. The path wriggles its way through this to reach open fields and then disappears. Head straight up the crest of the ridge towards the big tree to the left of the cottages. As you approach, you will see that there has been some alteration to field boundaries. A new fence has been erected, cutting off the top right-hand corner of the field. The enclosed area has been planted with trees. The map shows that the right of way runs through this new plantation. There is a stile, of sorts, in the fence, but its positioning near the telephone pole makes it very difficult to negotiate. There is no sign that any walker has used it, nor is there any sign of a path inside the plantation. There is a semblance of a path running alongside the new fence up to the track at the top of the hill.

An Old Main Road

This track was once a main road, the Blythe Marsh to Thorpe turnpike. At this point it is now little more than a track, though you can still drive a car on it if you wish. Turn right along the track, which soon passes through a gate and becomes a proper tarmac road. Just before the gate you will notice a footpath sign on the right, by a stile, directing you through the new plantation. This end of the path looks as little used as the other.

The road now enters the village of Thorpe and soon reaches the church on the right. As the name suggests, Thorpe is a Danish settlement, but the church is Norman. Just beyond the church, go right, down a narrow lane, which gives every indication of being a private drive. At the end of the lane, where it swings left to a house and garage, bear right onto a path which skirts round the bottom of the church yard. A short distance along this path, go sharply left, descending towards the valley bottom on a muddy and slippery, terraced track. Look out for a well-hidden stile on the right, only a few steps down the terraced path. This stile goes through a wall to deposit you in a steep open field. Make your way down the hillside to the stream, bearing right. Cross the stream and scramble up to the hedge, where there is a stile.

In this next field the path starts alongside the left-hand wall, then again bears right and rises steeply, heading for the second wall corner. When this corner is reached, you will see a gate and post in the wall ahead, by a cattle drinking trough. Go through the gate, not down the more obvious track. Once in the next field, make a bee-line for the farm ahead, keeping to the left of the clump of trees. There is no obvious path on the ground but the farm is a clear guide. Eventually, as you near the corner of the field, there is a stile in the wall on the left. Go through this and resume the line of march to the farm, to reach another stile, just to the left of the gate. Still head towards Spend Lane Farm, but do not go through the stile onto the road. Instead, continue in the field with the hedge on your left, skipping over the spring and its attendant boggy area, using the stepping stones thoughtfully provided. In this manner you reach a stile by a gate and an ash tree. A very narrow field now follows. This is exited by a stile next to the gate that leads onto the Mappleton road, just near its junction with Spend Lane.

Leaving The Park Behind

Cross the Mappleton road and go left at the stile by the footpath sign, which obligingly drops you into a quagmire. This can be skirted on the left by keeping close to the fence. After that a good track materialises and is followed. There are lovely views down the Dove Valley from here, as well as back up into the Peak. At a kink in the left-hand hedge, the track also turns left, but your path goes straight ahead. There is little evidence of the path on the ground but it soon crosses a shallow ditch which is shown on the OS map as a field boundary and as the National Park boundary. Beyond this remnant, the path bears left to reach a stile in the field corner, by an oak tree.

The path now follows the left-hand hedge through two fields, until a strip of woodland is encountered on the left. A stile leads into this and this is your route. Go through the strip of woodland, which is very narrow at this point and emerge into fields again. Ignore the sign post pointing to Mappleton and head across the field, bearing right towards the solitary ash. Continue ahead to a stile in the hedge by the oak tree. Straight on again to reach a gap in the far hedge. After that, the path follows the left-hand hedge through a field bearing all the signs of ridge and furrow farming, to reach a gap in the far corner, by an old stone post.

The path through this next field moves slowly away from the right-hand hedge to reach a stile to the right of two ash trees. In the next field, carry straight on, along the same alignment to a stile in the opposite hedge. Ignore paths going off left and right. The next field is very narrow, and rapidly crossed. The following field is broader, with a barn on the left-hand side. Go straight on to a stile near the gate by the ash tree. There is also a pond in the corner of this field, but the author did not stop to investigate the wildlife potential.

Back Onto The Tissington Trail

In the next field, keep the hedge to your left and continue in this manner into a second field. In this second field, ignore the gate in the left-hand hedge and continue almost to the corner of the field where there is a stile on the left. At this point, you are almost at Callow Top Farm and there is quite an extensive view over the valley of the Bentley Brook. The stile gives out onto the access lane to the farm and here you go left to descend the road. At the cattle-grid there is a stile, which should be used if you don't fancy a broken leg. Beyond this point, the road makes a bee-line for Haywood Farm just below. The path bears right however, leaving the road and keeping by the stream and hedge. It descends quite steeply to meet the lane again at another stile. Immediately ahead is the bridge carrying the Tissington Trail over the lane, but there is no access to the Trail at this point. The lane is left at once. Cross the stream by the bridge, to join a path on the right, accessed by a stile next to the gate. In the field, bear left to come alongside the former railway line.

Follow the fence on your left to reach a stile in the field corner. A flight of steps leads up onto the Trail. Here you turn right and follow the Trail back to Mappleton Lane Car Park, where, with any luck, the cycle hire centre will be open and serving soft drinks.

4: BARLOW

The Route: Barlow Church – Elm Tree Farm – Lee Bridge – Brind-woodgate – Cartledge – Holmesfield – Millthorpe – Johnnygate – Rumbling Street –Wildaygreen – Bolehill – Barlow

Distance: 6.1 miles (9.75km)

Start: Barlow Church, Grid reference: 345746

Map(s): OS 1:25000 Pathfinder Series No. 761 Chesterfield

How to get there:

By Public Transport: Monday to Saturday service from Chesterfield to Barlow. Seasonal Sunday service from Chesterfield. Daily service from Sheffield to Holmesfield, Monday to Saturday service from Chesterfield to Holmesfield.

By Car: B6051 from Chesterfield to Barlow, A621 from Sheffield to Owler Bar then B6051 to Barlow.

The Pub

The George and Dragon is opposite the church, on the main road in Holmesfield. It serves Wards fine malt ales on hand pump, as well as Vaux Best Bitter. There are two main rooms, a lounge bar and a public bar, neither of which is barred to walkers, though if you're wet and muddy you'd be better in the public room. Opening hours are 11am – 2pm and 4.30pm –11pm, Monday to Friday, 12noon – 4pm and 6pm – 11pm on Saturday, 12noon – 3pm and 8pm – 10.30pm on Sundays. Meals are served at lunchtimes and evenings and there's an outdoor seating area for the fresh air fanatics.

The Walk

The walk begins in Barlow, by the Norman church of St Lawrence. Barlow is a picturesque village, with a long established well dressing tradition. The wells are dressed using whole flower heads instead of the more common flower petals. The village name derives from the former land owners, the de Barley's, who held the manor from the time of the Norman Conquest. Robert Barley was the first husband of the famous Bess of Hardwick.

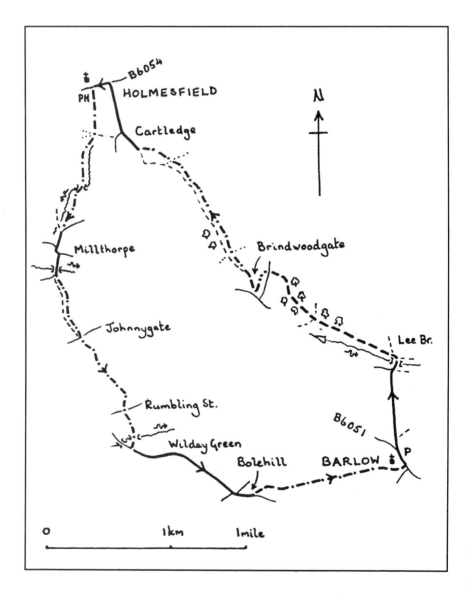

Along An Ancient Highway

From the church, walk along the road in the direction of Barlow Commonside. Cross the road and at the junction, where the main road bears left, go straight ahead along the narrow lane. This passes the entrance to Elm Tree Farm on the right and then begins to descend into the valley of the Barlow Brook. The woodland on the opposite side of the valley is Monk Wood. The lane soon becomes quite deeply sunken below the level of the surrounding fields. This is normally a sign of long and heavy use, as is the case here, for this was the old road to Dronfield. The lane drops through a tunnel of trees with a profusion of flowers on the banks in Spring, before reaching a junction with another lane. The road you are on now descends to cross the Barlow Brook and the tarred surface ceases at the bridge.

Just beyond the bridge there is a gate on the left leading to a path beside the river, but this is not the right of way. Continue up the rough lane for a short distance to a stile on the left, which is signed and which leads onto a narrow path through the wood. A pleasant stroll through a delightful mixed woodland now follows, with glimpses to the left, down to the stream and its attendant trout ponds. The path emerges from the wood at a stile and more ponds can be seen below and ahead. The path runs through an area of scrubby hawthorn and gorse, descending towards the ponds. However, where the path splits, keep right, heading away from the ponds to a waymarked gate which leads back into woodland again.

The path now rises away from the valley bottom and soon a crossing of routes is reached. Go straight on here, keeping quite close to the boundary of the wood on your left, until you reach a gate and stile. This takes you out of the wood onto a narrow hedged track, which soon leads onto the lane, near to Brindwoodgate. At the lane go right for a short distance, then left at the footpath sign into a rough and steep field. Go down the left-hand side of the field, which is so steep that at one point there are steps, and so find a stile in the hedge on the left. Go over this stile and then locate a further stile on the right, which drops you neatly into someone's back garden. Fear not, for this is the right of way. It skirts the right-hand edge of the garden to reach the drive, then ascends to a junction of drives/tracks, just before the road. Go right at the junction of tracks and thus enter a narrow lane. Continue up the lane a short way until you reach a white gate with a stile to the right. A glance at the OS map will show two parallel rights of way here, one a footpath, the other a bridleway. Either will do, for your purposes, but the footpath is the drier and has the more open views.

Go through the stile by the white gate and so enter fields. Keep close company with the hedge on the left, which segregates you from the bridleway and in this manner proceed through a couple of fields. There are no stiles, the boundary hedges being breached by wide gaps. Ignore a stile in the hedge on the left and continue ahead, still keeping close to the bridleway and passing under the electricity line. Ignore a gate in the hedge on the left and continue to ascend gently to reach a stile in the wall across your line of march. At this point while checking the walk, I was surprised to see a fox trot jauntily across the path, less than 25 yards ahead.

Beyond the stile carry on up by the side of the bridleway to a gate in the wall. This takes you into the bridleway, which at this point is on the same level as the path. However, you immediately leave the track by negotiating a waymarked chain stile on the right. The route strikes across the field, away from the bridleway, heading for the fourth tree from the left in a clump seen ahead. If you have followed these instructions you should come to a gate and stile. Ignore these and bear left, with the hedge on your right to reach another stile in the field corner. Negotiate this unusual stile (another chain stile) and continue ahead by the fence towards the solitary tree. Ignore the gate on the right, but follow the field boundary as it swings left to pass the farm and thus reaches a stile by the gate post.

Cartledge And Holmesfield

This neatly drops you back onto the bridleway again and here you turn right along the track, soon passing Cartledge Hall on the right. The track now becomes a tarred road and soon reaches a junction. Go straight on here, with an extensive view to the right, and so reach Holmesfield. At the junction with the B6054, go left to reach the George and Dragon. Holmesfield has no shortage of pubs. You'll pass no fewer than three before you reach the chosen one. Some people may find this too great a temptation, but be warned; You have barely done half the walk! Holmesfield is an ancient village. Domesday records the manor as being held by the Deincourt family, but it passed into the hands of the Cavendishes in the reign of Edward the Sixth. There are still a number of fine old buildings, including the 17th century hall.

On leaving the George and Dragon, turn right and at the end of the pub go right again, down a narrow lane past a good stone built "thunderbox". You soon reach a gate and stile which takes you into open fields, with a lovely view to the right towards the moors near Owler Bar. Keep alongside the hedge to the next set of gates. There is a slight hiatus here, for the gates are also used as sheep pens and may be difficult to open. Having extricated yourself from the pens, continue down by the hedge to a stile in the bottom corner of the field. In the next field, the path roughly follows the hedge on the left, down to a multi-armed signpost. Continue down the field following the sign to Millthorpe. At the bottom of this field there is a stile which leads into a lovely old fashioned hay meadow, brim full of flowers in Spring. On you go, down the field with the stream to your left. Ignore the gate on the left and continue down until you reach a stile and bridge. Cross the stream and continue merrily downhill with the brook now on your right. The next two boundary hedges are breached by gaps and have no stiles, but the path keeps on the top of the stream bank. Keep a sharp look out for bulls in these fields. They have a nasty habit of being hidden behind the hedge and the gaps mean that the only safe exit is a flying leap over the stream!

Millthorpe

Having avoided the bull, you reach a gate and stile and drop into a narrow hollow-way. This soon leads out onto the road. Turn right here and thus reach Millthorpe. The Royal Oak at Millthorpe features in "More Pub Walks in the Peak District" so you'll have to obtain that book for details. It's well worth visiting however. Go straight over at the crossroads and descend the little lane to the right of the cafe. This soon reaches the ford and bridge over the Millthorpe Brook. The ford is not usually a problem and may be a useful way to remove mud, but the surface is slippery. Perhaps the bridge is preferable after all.

The road deteriorates to a rough track beyond the ford and a footpath goes off to the right. Ignore this and carry on up the track until it also bears right, heading towards the farm buildings. There is a choice of routes here. Straight ahead is the very narrow and well-used bridleway, quite steep in parts and very muddy and slippery in others. You can use this route but it is not advised. To the right there is a signed footpath into the fields. This is not your route at all. To the left of the bridleway is a stile and this is the recommended route. It is another example of two parallel rights of way, very similar to that encountered at the start of the walk. Once over the stile turn right and keep by the hedge to a stile and bridge over the delightfully named Pingle Dike. Another stile takes you

back into fields again. There is little or no evidence on the ground of this
path, but if you keep alongside the boundary hedge and fence on the
right you cannot go far wrong. You get occasional glimpses down into
the bridleway which is very deep in places. Ignore any gates and gaps
leading into the hollow-way but continue upwards, by the hedge, to a
stile at the top of the field. Beware frisky horses! Still keeping close to
the right-hand side of the field, skirt the shed and pause for a breather,
and for a look back over Holmesfield. A grand view. Just past the shed
there is a gate ahead and this brings you back onto the bridleway just at
Johnnygate Farm. Straight ahead is the road.

Go right at the road and then at once left, over a stile signposted to
Oxton Rakes. Once in the field go straight ahead with the barn and
hedge to your left. Another stile quickly follows and in this field the
indistinct path runs alongside the left-hand hedge. The author had to
sprint at this point when checking the walk, because of a disturbing
combination of a frisky stallion and a cow with calf. Like the fields near
Millthorpe, the hedge here is broken with gaps and there is no escape
until you leap over the stile into the wood. The path then bears right
through the wood, to cross a stone bridge and thus reach another stile
which leads into fields again. Keep alongside the right-hand hedge and
fence by the wood, to a gateway. After that, the path continues with the
hedge to the left, through a couple of fields to a gateway by a culverted
stream. The path, now a broad track, then ascends through a cutting,
bearing right, then left to reach the gateway at the entrance to Rumbling
Street Farm. There is a good view back towards Holmesfield from here.
Go through the gate and through the farm, with the barn on your left
and the farmhouse on the right, to reach the road.

Crowhole Reservoir and Bolehill

Cross the road and go over the signposted stile into fields again. There is
a view ahead and left, to Bolehill, which you have yet to climb. Go down
the field with the wall and hedge on your left to reach a stile by the oak
tree. The stretch of water seen on the right is Crowhole Reservoir. Still
head down the next field with the hedge to the left until it swings
sharply away. There is a convincing looking track following the hedge
line down to the stream, but this has been made by four footed walkers.
The footpath bears right at this point, dropping steeply down towards
the stream, where a quick sideways shuffle round a waymarked tree
reveals a bridge. Cross the bridge and head up the field on the far side
to a stile hidden behind the holly tree. This deposits you on the road and
here you turn left.

Follow the road uphill, past Spout Farm and Holme Farm, ignoring footpath signs leading off left, until the "cross roads" is reached. Continue past Wildacre, on the route signed to Barlow, which leads up to the notch in the top of Bolehill. As usual this place-name denotes an old smelting site. The smelters relied on natural wind power to provide the draught for their furnaces, so Bolehills are usually windy, exposed places. This one is no exception. Just opposite the driveway to Bolehill Nursery, go left along the driveway to Bolehill House. Where the drive swings left into the garden, go straight ahead, through a waymarked gate and follow the overgrown beech hedge, past the old seat on the left, to another gate. Here the track finishes and you are in open fields. There is an extensive view from this point, right over Chesterfield to Bolsover and beyond.

The Back Way into Barlow

The path follows the right-hand edge of the field and, although the map shows the right of way clipping off the corner, the walked line continues by the hedge to the end of the field. Then turn left to reach a stile in the boundary on the right. From this point the path follows the top of the ridge down towards Barlow, with wide views to the north, east and south. Head towards the solitary tree, straight across the middle of the field and thus locate a stile. Again the route lies straight ahead, now heading for the white house. In the next boundary there is a stile by the gate and the path goes down the mid field again, though keeping nearer to the right-hand edge, heading for a stile and gate. The tower of Barlow church is now in view ahead and is a useful marker. The path continues this straight course through a couple more fields, each with stile in the right places, until it reaches the wall surrounding the churchyard. The path becomes a farm track, does a crafty right and left between the church and the farm yards and thus reaches the main road in Barlow village.

5: BELPER

The Route: Belper Bridge – Chevin Green – Chevin Mount – Farnah Green – Deeps of Lumb – Blackbrook – Longwalls Lane – Belper Lane End – Wyver Farm – Scotches – Belper Bridge

Distance: 5.25 miles (8.3km). Allow two – two and a half hours, excluding pub stop. To/from Belper railway station is half a mile extra (0.9km) each way

Start: Belper Bridge, Grid reference: 345482

Map(s): OS 1:25000 Pathfinder Series No. 811 Belper

How to get there:

By Public Transport: Good daily bus services from Derby, Manchester, Nottingham and various other towns. The bus station is in the town centre, but certain services stop at the Triangle, which is near Belper Bridge. Daily train service from Derby and Matlock to station in town centre.

By Car: A6 from north or south, A517 from Ashbourne direction. Various car parks in the town. Very limited parking near the bridge.

The Pub

The Bulls Head at Belper Lane End, is a fine free house serving Bass beers and food daily. It stands on the old main road out of Belper to the north. It keeps the usual opening hours and has an outdoor seating area for the walker who is too mean to buy a sandwich.

The Walk

Go over the bridge from the town on the A517 road. Just on the north side of the bridge, go left onto a path by the river. This first part is almost like a promenade, with a hard surface and railings between you and the river. There is a good view back up river to the bridge, the weir and the impressive Belper East Mills. The original mills were founded by

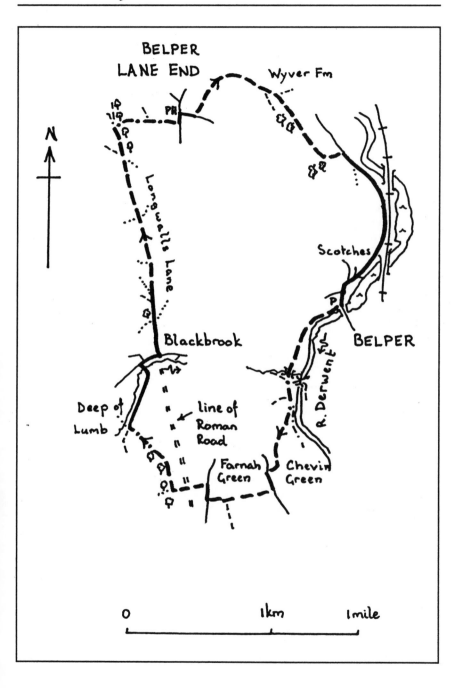

Messrs Arkwright and Strutt in 1776. Many mill buildings and workers' cottages associated with this period still survive in the town. Even before the Industrial Revolution, Belper was a noted industrial town, being famed for its nail manufacturing. In Georgian times the town expanded greatly and the main street contains some attractive buildings of this era.

The "prom" soon relapses into a normal footpath as you go over a stile just to the right of a small building. A pleasant walk through fields by the river then follows, with a wall on your left and a good view to the right up to Chevinside. After another stile the path crosses a bridge over a small stream. Note the wall on the left, which is pierced with holes to allow the flood water to pass through. Making a mental note not to try this walk in a cloud-burst, carry on along the path to a gate with a stile on either side. Take your pick, but once over, carry straight on by the fence, crossing a track.

Leave the Riverbank

Carry on along an indistinct path, keeping to the left of the gateposts and ignoring the gate and stile on your right. Your route now bears left to come alongside the river. It is easy to go wrong here, as the riverside walk is so obvious and delightful, but after 150 yards, keep your eyes peeled for a stile and gate in the hedge on the right. Once you find this, go over the stile and bear left, heading across the field, (not straight up it), following an obvious cattle track.

The track passes through a gap in the wall and continues to slant up the next field, passing a spring on the left. The views across the Derwent to Belper are increasingly good as height is gained. The track now goes through a gap in a hedge and bears left, rising more steeply.

In this next field, which has a few scrubby hawthorns, the path is paved, though the paving is well hidden under the grass in places. The path reaches the wall corner at the top of the rise, at the backs of the houses of Chevin Green. At the wall corner, the path goes sharp right, through a stile at the right-hand end of the barbed wire fence. This takes you onto a private drive, but there is a public footpath down to the Chevin Road. At the road go left.

On Chevin Mount

Continue along the road almost to the next house, to a signposted stile on the right. Go over the stile and into fields again, to begin the ascent of

Chevin Mount. The climb is quite steep, but mercifully brief. The path follows the wall all the way up, through a couple of stiles to eventually emerge on North Lane. This is a good place to stop and catch your breath and claim that you are looking at the view. The view is very good across the valley to Belper and Crich. Belper's name derives from the Norman French "Beaurepaire" and you can see why when you gaze across the valley. The settlement was originally part of a royal hunting forest and there are charters to the town dating back to the 12th and 13th centuries. Some distance to the left, along North Lane, is the Chevin Tower. It was built in 1839 as a sighting tower for surveyors involved in the driving of Milford railway tunnel. It also seems to have housed machinery used in the sinking of the adjacent ventilation shaft. "Chevin" is derived from the Welsh *cefn*, meaning 'ridge'; an apt name.

At North Lane, go right and follow the track as it swings sharply left and descends to Farnah Green. If you're in need of refreshment, there is the Blue Bell Inn just to the left, which has a beer garden and welcomes walkers. If you're not going to the pub, go right at the road and in about 100 yards, just past the bus stop, go left up what appears to be a drive to a bungalow. It is also a public footpath and is signed as such. There are two drives here, side by side. Yours is the left-hand one.

The path skirts the bungalow to a stile by a gate. It crosses a track, which is actually the other driveway, to a further stile by another gate. In the next field the path imperceptibly crosses the line of the Roman Road, which you will meet later as Longwalls Lane. The course of the road is marked by a wall and a belt of trees.

Descent of The Deeps of Lumb

Continue ahead by a wall to a stile, well hidden in a clump of holly. Negotiate this and enter Lumb Wood. The land falls away steeply in the wood into the Deeps of Lumb. The place name "lumb" means a steep sided wooded valley, a very apt description in this instance. The path bears right and begins to descend gently, keeping to the top side of the wood. On the left the land falls steeply through deciduous jungle to Lumb Brook. In places the path runs through a virtual tunnel of trees and shrubs, finally crossing a couple of stiles to emerge into open fields again. Ahead can be seen the mast crowned Alport Hill.

The path bears left, heading diagonally down the field to a stile in the far hedge, to the right of the big tree. In the next field, bear left again to a stile which takes you into a narrow lane. Here go right.

The lane sees very little traffic and rapidly takes you down to the ford a Blackbrook. If your boots are muddy, here's the opportunity to clean them, but beware, the ford is slippery underfoot and there's nothing worse than walking in soaking clothes. Better use the footbridge provided and so ascend to the main A517 road, turning right by the telephone box.

Go along the main road, keeping to the footway. Pass Plains Lane on the left and then at Longwalls Lane go left.

A Fine Stretch of Roman Road

Longwalls Lane is the longest and steepest climb of the walk and it should be taken steadily. The first section, up to the drive of Holly House, is simply a rough road which belies its historic origins. If you pause, (and you will), and look back across the valley, you will see a line of trees on the same alignment as the lane. Further down, in the field below the trees, two straight lines show up in certain lights, the boundary ditches of the former Roman Road mentioned earlier. Longwalls Lane is a continuation of that road and despite its present appearance has probably been in continuous use for close on 2000 years. The "walls" element of the Longwalls place name is often indicative of a Roman route, the word being a corruption of the Latin "vallum".

Continue up the lane, passing the driveway to the porticoed Holly House, with its monkey puzzle trees. This house was built by the Slater family. Samuel Slater was apprentice to Jedidiah Strutt at Belper Mills. Slater emigrated to America where he put his apprenticeship to good use, being regarded as the "Father of American Manufactury". Another relation, Thomas Slater of Chapel Farm, was known as Parson Slater. He built the methodist chapel at Shottle, where Wesley preached on occasion. Beyond Holly House the lane becomes even rougher and beyond Starbuck House it narrows still further, but is still used by horses and cyclists.

Continue upwards, the views constrained by the fact that the lane is sunken and the boundary walls are on the top of the cutting. However, now and then there are pleasant glimpses to the right over to Belper and to the left towards Shottle. For the most part, this section is shaded with trees, but as the gradient eases you emerge from cover. Now the view is extensive, particularly southwards, to the Trent power stations and Cannock Chase. Northwards the view is still constrained, though Alport Hill is prominent. It is surprising from how far away Alport Hill can be seen. It was an important marker on the Saxon Portway, an early north south route which utilised Longwalls Lane. The exploration of the Portway route from Derby northwards makes for a rewarding long distance walk.

Continue along the sandy track and soon reach another track going off to the left and signed as a footpath. Ignore this and carry straight on. Beyond this point Longwalls Lane widens and is used by farm vehicles. Soon you will reach another footpath sign on the right. Go right here, through the stile and into a narrow field. The path goes straight across the field to another stile which leads you into a thin belt of trees. There are paths left and right in the wood but ignore these and continue straight ahead, descending to a stile, which even boasts a hand rail.

Belper Lane End and Wyver Farm

Emerging from the wood, you can see Belper Lane End and the pub just below, with Ambergate and Crich to the left and over the valley. The path now descends rapidly, with the wall on the left, to reach a stile by a gate. Here the path becomes a narrow walled lane which soon reaches the road known as Dalley Lane. Here go left and so reach the Bulls Head at Belper Lane End.

On leaving the pub, go straight ahead down Belper Lane. By the first house on the left, go left, through a signed gate and take the little used bridleway towards Wyver Farm. The bridleway describes a graceful arc around the northern and western flanks of Wyver Hill, keeping close to the wall on the left. It passes through three gates, with no attendant stiles, before reaching Wyver Farm. Another gate takes you into the farm complex and here the track forks. Go straight on through the farmyard, ignoring the inevitable dog. Once through the farm, there is a fine view over the Derwent to Broadholm.

Follow the walled track as it slopes gently down towards the river. The track goes through a gate into open fields and then swings left to another gate, where Wyver Lane is joined. Go right here.

Wyver Lane is a proper tarmac road, but you'll not be unduly inconvenienced by traffic. There are lovely glimpses of the Derwent, and, for the railway enthusiast, the Derby – Sheffield main line comes very close at one point. The railway eventually leaves the road to cross the Derwent and there are then views across the broad river to the Belper Mills. The river here has been dammed, hence its width – in order to provide water power for the mills. It has created a most attractive area, a good example of the way some industrial processes can enhance a landscape.

A Brave Man Indeed

Soon the first cottages are reached, with the buildings on the right-hand side of the road and their gardens on the left. The area has the curious name of Scotches. The owner of the first cottage is a brave man, for he has put up a Great Western Railway notice on his property, here in the heart of Midland Railway territory.

At the junction with Belper Lane, go left and so join the main A517, Ashbourne – Belper road, just on the North side of Belper Bridge. Straight on over the bridge to the town and the railway station.

6: BENTLEY HALL

The Route: Bentley Hall – Meadow Hayes Farm – Boylestone Chapel –Rose and Crown – Riddings Farm – Cubley Carr – Little Cubley – Coppice Farm – Bentley Hall

Distance: 4.7 miles (7.5km)

Start: Bentley Hall, Grid reference: 177381

Map(s): OS 1:25000 Pathfinder Series No. 831 Uttoxeter

How to get there:

By Public Transport: There is a very sparse bus service to Boylestone. There are no buses at all on Mondays and Sundays and none any day of the week to Bentley Hall.

By Car: A515 from Ashbourne or Sudbury. Take the turning to Alkmonton and Great Cubley at Cubley cross roads, by the Howard Arms. Bentley Hall is about 2 miles (3.2 km) beyond Great Cubley.

The Pub

The pub is the Rose and Crown at Boylestone. It is a delightfully unspoilt country inn. In the tiny bar you'll be assured of a warm welcome, especially if it is winter and the open fire is blazing away! You'll also encounter a lively atmosphere and a grand drop of Bass. If something stronger is your tipple, then the landlord prides himself on the pub's selection of whiskies. He also provides live vocal/piano entertainment on Friday and Saturday evenings. Opening hours are 12noon – 3pm and 5pm – 11pm Monday to Friday, (closed Tuesday lunchtimes), 12noon – 4pm and 7pm – 11pm on Saturday, 12noon – 3pm and 7pm – 10.30pm on Sundays. Rolls and soup are served daily, but for the sandwich-toting walker, there's a large beer garden round the back of the pub. However, on cold days in winter the lure of the "real" fires in the bar and snug will prove irresistible.

The Rose and Crown

The Walk

The walk starts by going through a gate about 100 metres on the Cubley side of Bentley Hall. There is neither signpost nor stile, but there is a fairly obvious track. Oddly, after you have walked along the track for a short distance there is a footpath sign, seemingly out of place and quite useless from a navigational point of view. Continue ahead, making your way in intrepid fashion, through the sheep pens which block the right of way.

The track continues ahead with the hedge or fence on your right. Pass through the gateway and continue alongside the fence, passing a depression on the right which might have been an old pond or a shallow quarry. Another gateway follows, the path still keeping alongside the right-hand fence, to reach a further gateway by a trough.

Meadow Hayes Farm

Head now for a gate to the right of the pond and clump of trees. This gate proves difficult to open. In the next field there are apparently two stiles in the fence ahead, but when you get closer you will find that they

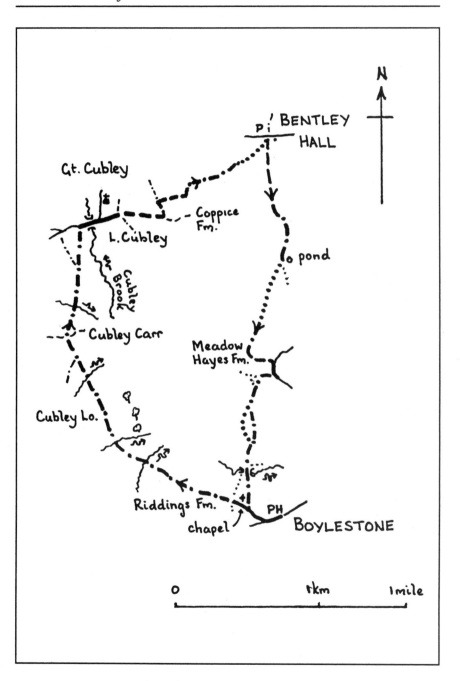

are on either side of a fenced farm track. Negotiate these stiles and then
head for the two trees in the middle of the field. Meadow Hayes Farm is
now in view ahead and this, too, is a good marker. Follow the line of
pylons down to the fence noting with some dismay that there is no stile,
so some undignified scrambling is called for. Continue straight ahead
following the shallow depression in the field. At the next fence there is
again no stile. More agility called for. Keep the hedge on your left in the
next field and to your surprise you will find a stile in the far boundary.
You are now fast approaching Meadow Hayes Farm. Just before the
farm, there is a gate on the right, but this is not the route you want.
Continue to the second gate, which is waymarked and which leads you
into the farmyard. Pass through the farmyard, with the house on your
right and join the driveway down to the lane.

An Interesting Navigational Exercise

At the lane, go right and continue to descend until you reach a footpath
sign on the right, just before the white house. Turn sharply right at this
point and follow the deeply sunken lane, past the house and up to a
gate, which just about opens. Continue up the lane until it ends at two
gates. According to the map, the right-hand gate is the route of the right
of way. You are welcome to try it. The author did and found no means
of extricating himself from the field. Go through the left-hand gate
instead, then head across the field, to the left of the solitary hawthorn
and clump of bushes. In this manner you will join a hedge on your left
and you should then follow this down the field.

The map shows that the right of way should be on the opposite side of
the hedge, but I defy you to find a way through until you reach the gate
by the oak tree, about half way down the field. Go through the gate and
turn right, still following the hedge. Despite your rising doubts about the
author's route descriptions and ability to find paths, you will be gratified
to learn that, at the bottom of this field there is a stile. You will be less
pleased to discover that the stile is defended by a ditch. Follow the field
boundary as it kinks first left, then right, then left again. Thus you come
to a fence, which would be easy to negotiate were it not for the fact that
some kind soul has strung a length of barbed wire across. With reasonable agility this can be surmounted and you continue through the next
field with the hedge on your left, to reach a gap in the far corner.

There is some evidence that other walkers avoid the section between the
gate by the oak and this point, by making a bee-line across the interven-
ing fields. Certainly, when you reach the gap there is evidence of a stile

of sorts in the hedge on the left. However, your route is shown on the map as the right of way. Turn right at the gap and follow the right-hand hedge, veering away from it to reach the bridge, half hidden by willow trees. In the next field, head towards the left of Riddings Farm, seen ahead, to reach a gate just by the Methodist Chapel. Here you join a narrow little lane and go left to reach the "main" road. One hundred metres to the left lies the pub.

Boylestone

Boylestone village lies a little further on than the pub. It contains an interesting 14th century church, with a fine pyramid roofed tower. In 1664, during the Civil War a group of 200 Royalist soldiers, en route to the relief of Wingfield Manor, made an overnight stop in the church. Unfortunately for them they failed to mount a guard and were surrounded by a troop of Parliamentary soldiers and forced to surrender, mercifully without a shot being fired.

On leaving the pub, retrace your steps to the Methodist Chapel. This tiny little building in an isolated spot, was erected in 1846. It is quite surprising to see it still in use, many of these small chapels having been closed in recent years. Bear left past the chapel and continue along the lane, past the farm until you reach a gate into the fields.

Another Interesting Bit of Navigation

This point has a number of paths crossing and can be confusing. Do not go through the gateway on the right, but bear left, heading up towards the building near the further end of the field. Follow the fence/hedge to reach a gate in the hedge ahead, by the holly tree. Continue ahead to reach another gate, with no accompanying stile. Continue on the same general alignment and you will come up against a fence across the line of march. Here there is neither gate nor stile, but there is a large gap in the right-hand fence. You should ignore the gap and negotiate the fence instead, continuing then alongside the right-hand fence. The path begins to skirt to the left of an old quarry. There is a stile on the right leading into the worked out area, but this is of no use to you and doesn't appear on the map as a right of way. Go past the quarry and carry straight on to reach a big gate to the right of a trough. Head diagonally left across the next field, towards the large ash tree. The left-hand hedge is then followed to a stile, just to the right of the field corner. Cross the stream by the bridge thoughtfully provided, though cursing the generous growth of nettles. Then proceed up alongside the left-hand hedge, with some considerable new tree planting on the left. The woodland on the right is Beryl's Gorse, though who Beryl was and why she wanted a gorse plantation is not recorded. On the left is Cubley Lodge, alongside the main A515 road.

A further nettle infested bridge soon follows, complete with waymarked stile. Keep straight on, crossing the track to Cubley Lodge and keeping to the left of the new fence, which defends a new pond from approach. You will spot three big trees ahead. The gate you want is between the first and second tree from the left. There is no stile again, but the gate is easily negotiated. Straight on now, heading towards Cubley Carr, which is the house by the poplar trees in view ahead. The next stile is in the far right-hand corner of the field, by the electricity pole. It is waymarked, but that is no defence against the inevitable crop of nettles, which contest the approach to the bridge. Once over the bridge, follow the right-hand hedge up towards the house and thus reach the farm access road. Go right here, then almost at once turn left, leaving the farm road through a gate, to skirt round to the left of the silo.

Beware of The Bull!

Once past the silo, Cubley Church comes into view ahead. Descend to the piece of corrugated metal in the far fence and hedge, by the willow tree. This is what passes for a stile. The approach is muddy and the balancing act required demands a fair degree of agility. Straight on from here, by the waymarked oak tree and its attendant gate. Still going straight on you reach another gate in a newly defined field. A cattle track then heads across towards Cubley church to reach a stile just to the left of the bridge. When this walk was reconnoitred, there was a large bull in this field. Admittedly he was with a herd of cows, but discretion decided that a deviation should be used, especially as the herd was clustered round the exit stile. Fortunately, as the map shows, there is another path, which leaves the cattle track just after the gate and bears left towards the houses and the Howard Arms, by the main road. A stile leads up to the minor road to Little Cubley. Whichever stile you use, you will join the same lane and you should then turn right.

Cubley

Cross the bridge over Cubley Brook and then the second bridge over the mill stream. Cubley Mill Farm is on the right. At the cross roads, by the seat, go straight on, up the hill, with the church to your left. St Andrew's church is 12th – 13th century, but there is mention of a church here in

Domesday Book. Opposite the church stood the manor house of the local gentry the Montgomerys. The house and the family have long gone but their memorials remain in the church and the churchyard. Michael Johnson, the father of the famous Dr. Samuel Johnson, hailed from Cubley before moving to Lichfield as a book seller.

The lane soon forks, the left-hand route going to the old Rectory, your route going straight on, despite the Private signs. You will see a footpath sign to the right, but this is of no consequence to you. Continue up along the lane towards Coppice Farm. Just before the farm buildings are reached, go left alongside the hedge, with the trees that presumably gave the farm its name on your right. At the gateway in the corner of the field, by the electricity junction pole, go right, still following the boundary of the farm enclosure. The author was molested by sheep (!) in this field when trying out the walk. An interesting experience. At the far end of the field there are a gate and stile which are quickly scaled to avoid any more amorous attentions from the sheep.

In this next field, which is very narrow, bear left to a gate near the holly tree. Then continue ahead straight across the middle of the next field, heading to the right of the clump of trees. Bentley Hall is now in view ahead. At the far side of the field there is a stile by an oak tree. Now bear left across the next field, keeping just to the right of the far corner of the wood. Once past the wood, continue to bear left to reach a gate by the solitary ash tree. The gate turns out to be a combination of gate plus bridge, plus second gate. Nearly back now. Go straight on towards the hall, keeping to the right of the clump of thorns and so reach the track on which you set out earlier. It is important to turn left at this point, otherwise you'll go all the way round again!

7: BRADLEY

The Route: Bradley – Bradley Pastures – Corley Farm – Ridge Lane –Atlow – Dayfield Farm – Gorse Lane – Fox and Hounds – Lower Hough Park –Crowtrees – Bradley

Distance: 4.4 miles (7km)

Start: Bradley Village, by telephone box. Grid reference: 225458

Map(s): OS 1:25000 Pathfinder Series No. 811 Belper

How to get there:

By Public Transport: Monday to Saturday bus service from Derby, Belper and Ashbourne to The Jinglers/Fox and Hounds. No service to Bradley.

By Car: A517 from Belper or Ashbourne. Bradley is signed from A517. Limited parking by the telephone box in the middle of the village.

The Pub

This is a most unusual pub, in that it has two names, both of which are displayed on the inn sign. Apparently it is one of only two pubs in the country to have two official names. If you are approaching from Ashbourne, the pub is called The Jinglers, but if you're coming from Belper it is the Fox and Hounds. Apparently the Jinglers name derives from the existence of a toll gate by the pub. Coaches had to stop and ring a bell pull to attract the toll keeper's attention. The Jinglers/Fox and Hounds, serves a fine pint of Marstons and there are often guest beers as well. Opening hours are 11am – 2.30pm Monday to Saturday, 12noon – 3pm and 7pm – 10.30pm on Sundays. Food is served at lunchtimes and evenings and for the staying visitor there's self catering accommodation or a small caravan site. There are picnic tables and children's play area outside. Avoid leaning too far over the well and keep a sharp look-out for the two heifers, the peacock, guinea fowl, ducks, chickens and Christopher Columbus. (He's a rabbit by the way).

The Walk

From the centre of the village by the school and the telephone box, head up the lane towards the church. The church stands by itself on the left-hand side of the road, opposite Bradley Hall. It is dedicated to All Saints and is a peculiar building. The walls of the Nave show signs of having been raised, as the upper stone work is very different and so are the upper windows. The roof is virtually flat and there is neither tower nor spire, giving an unfinished effect. There was once a wooden bell tower, but it was destroyed in a thunderstorm. The main part of the church is 14th century, but there are the remains of a much older cross in the churchyard and inside there is a 13th century font. Bradley Hall used to stand on the same side of the road as the church, but the original building was demolished in the 18th century and the stable block converted into a new hall. Go past the church and continue along the road until you reach Hall Farm. The road through Bradley used to be the main road between Ashbourne and Derby, before the turnpike was built. Thus you walk in the steps of the Young Pretender, who passed this way in 1745.

Almost opposite Hall Farm is a gateway and cattle-grid. There is a pedestrian gate alongside, so in the interests of avoiding a broken leg at

Bradley Hall

this stage of the walk, use this and enter the field. A track leads to a row of cottages, but the footpath leaves the track at once and heads across the field to a gap at the right-hand end of the buildings. This gap takes you into another field. Head now towards the large white house. There is a gate in the left-hand corner of the field, and this has to be negotiated. It is so positioned as to act as a stile, but it will open, (unlike many on this walk). In the next field head again towards the white house, to a stile in the far left-hand corner. Go through this stile and onto the A517.

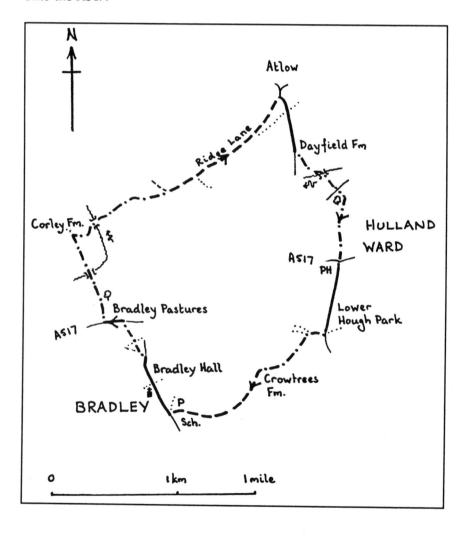

Of Nettles and Barbed Wire

The A517 is a busy and fast road, so cross it with care and go left, past the buildings of Bradley Pastures. Keep on the verge and ignore tempting driveways leading off to the right. Beyond the last of these, there is a footpath sign by a gate. There is no stile, but the gate opens to admit you into a field. The map shows the path heading to the left of the clump of trees ahead, but you first have to negotiate a fence which has materialised since the map was printed. Fortunately, there is a gate in the fence. Unfortunately, it shows a marked reluctance to open. Go over it and turn right heading towards the trees. There is a good view from here to the left towards Ashbourne. At the left-hand end of the trees there is another gate, which is equally reluctant to open and has to be scaled. Once over this gate, bear right through another gateway, which thankfully has no gate at all, and then turn left to head down the field towards Corley Farm, seen ahead. The view is extensive.

Continue down the field, with the hedge and ditch on your left and with a growing doubt in your mind about the way out. At the far end of the field there should be a stile, but of course there isn't. Nor is there an obvious gate, but others have passed this way before, and the wire fence is less fearsome in the corner. Climb over and, roundly cursing footpath blocking farmers, carry on through the next field to a substantial footbridge over the brook in the bottom left-hand corner. The bridge is defended by a generous growth of nettles, so shorts would not be advisable on this walk!

A Saga of Unopening Gates

The next field slopes up quite sharply and the far boundary cannot be seen. There is no evidence of a path on the ground, but there is an electricity line across your path. If you head in between the two big pylons, i.e. straight on, up the middle of the field, you will soon spot a gate, to the left of a small brick hut. As you will guess, the gate is of the unopening variety and has to be climbed. Corley Farm is straight ahead. The map shows the path performing a peculiar zig-zag in this field, which heads to the right-hand end of a barn. It then turns sharp right, almost a hairpin, to reach the field boundary you have just come through, then goes left to cross the stream. Logic would suggest an instant right turn as soon as you have climbed the gate, but the farm is too close for that and there is no evidence that others have done likewise, so head for the barn. Near the barn go sharp right and downwards along a faint terrace which soon reaches an equally sharp left-hand bend. Still descending, the path plunges into thick bushes and scrub, in the midst of which is the stream. There are neither bridge, nor stepping stones and some bright spark has strung a barbed wire fence along the opposite bank. However, the supporting posts have the merit of providing a reasonably secure hand hold to enable the brook to be crossed, and again there is some evidence that others have used the route before, as the wire is severed.

Having crossed the stream, and emerged from the bushes on the far bank, head up the field, not through the gateway on the right or along the obvious track to the left. Passing to the left of a clump of hawthorns you will discover a stile in the top hedge. Continue up the next field with a shallow depression and the hedge on your right to another gate, (the stile was an aberration). It is par for the course now that the gate does not open, and this one lives up to expectations. Carry on up the next field, still with the hedge on your right, gradually climbing onto a broad ridge with good views each side and behind. There is strong evidence that this was originally an old road. This explains the zig-zag approach to the stream near Corley Farm and the broad shallow trough by the hedge as the path climbed away from the stream. Eventually after a couple more gates, one of which opens, an armless signpost is reached and the path is joined from the left by a cart track.

Sprint Along Ridge Lane to Atlow

Continue up the ridge, along the track, still with the hedge on your right, to another gate. Miraculously this opens and leads you into a walled green lane of classic proportions. This is the appropriately named Ridge Lane. On the left is the valley of the Henmore Brook. It is flowing southwest. On the right is the Dayfield Brook, which is flowing north east!

Carry on along Ridge Lane at a cracking pace; the gradient is never severe, until you reach the road proper at Atlow. Atlow is a small hamlet sited on the Henmore Brook. It has a lovely Victorian church, the work of the local Derby architect H. I. Stevens. At the road turn right and continue along the lane towards Dayfield Farm. Just beyond the farm, there is a footpath sign on the left and there is also a stile in the hedge. Go over the stile into the field, then bear right to go diagonally across to try a find an exit in the far corner. There is a semblance of a stile a short way up the hedge from the corner. It is easy to see, but more difficult to climb. Beyond this "stile", bear right again and cross the corner of the field to the footbridge.

On the opposite side of the footbridge go straight up the field, heading to the left-hand end of the clump of trees on the horizon and following the remains of an old field boundary, now marked only by one or two big trees. These lead unerringly to a stile in the hedge at the top of the field. The stile steps are unsafe and in the final stages of disintegration, while the hedge is of hawthorn. Gorse Lane lies beyond the stile.

A Vanishing Path and Snowberry Bushes

Cross Gorse Lane and go down the roughly tarmaced track opposite. It is signed as a public footpath and passes an interesting collection of rotting farm lorries on the left. On the right is a small wood, and the map shows the path turning right at the far end of the trees. It does, but then rapidly deteriorates, eventually vanishing altogether in a riot of brambles and other bushes. The walked line continues into the field instead of turning right at the end of the wood. Then turn right and walk down the field alongside the hedge. The thickness of the hedge and occasional glimpses into it show that the path must at one time have been a narrow lane. It's now completely overgrown. A hedge is reached across the line of march. There is a ditch to be crossed but it's not difficult and there is an obvious gap in the hedge. The A517 is now only one field away. Keep by the hedge on your right and when almost at the road there is a gap which takes you back onto the true line of the path. The roadside footpath sign can be seen peering over a thicket of snowberry. It is easy to force a passage through these and emerge onto the road opposite the pub. (There is also a gap in the roadside hedge which avoids the snowberries, but purists will at least want to emerge onto the road at the correct point).

Careful Route Finding Needed

On leaving the pub, go down the lane past the well. After 400 yards, you pass a footpath sign on the right. The lane dips gently down to cross the Hulland Hollow Brook, then rises again to pass Lower Hough Park on the left. Just beyond Lower Hough Park there is another footpath sign on the right, pointing through a gateway. Go through the gateway and you are confronted by another gate to the left of an old railway waggon body. This gate opens and allows you into a small enclosure with rough buildings on the left. There is another gate at the far end of the enclosure. This also opens and lets you out into the field. It is easy to go wrong at this point and the author confesses to having done so while checking out this walk. You should ignore the tempting gateway, away to the left, and keep right instead, following a shallow depression to the corner of the field.

At the corner there is a stile on the left and a partly blocked gateway to the right, with an upturned sink to act as a step. Go over the left-hand stile and then bear left, diagonally across the field to reach a gateway beside a large ash tree.

Crowtrees Farm and Back to Bradley

Crowtrees Farm is now in view ahead and the path proceeds straight across the next field to a gate on the left of the holly tree. Negotiate the gate and turn right to reach the farm.

As you enter the small field next to Crowtrees Farm, the map implies that the path runs up the middle of the field with the farm on the left, then turns left along the fence line at the far end to reach the farmyard gate. At this point, there are two gates very close together and these have to be negotiated to enter the farmyard between two barns. The route then goes alongside the right-hand barn and exits the farm yard by a broad cart track on the right, to a modern working gate!

The cart track winds its way unerringly through a series of fields, eventually crossing a cattle-grid and becoming an enclosed lane. At the second cattle-grid the tarmac surface starts and the lane swings left to emerge in the centre of Bradley village, alongside the school and telephone box.

The Jinglers, or Fox and Hounds

8: CLOWNE

The Route: Clowne – Oxcroft Est. – Damsbrook – Border Lane – Markland Grips – Hollin Hill Road – Clowne Linear Park – Clowne

Distance: 4 miles (6.5 km)

Start: Car Park in centre of village, on the Elmton road just by District Council Offices. Grid reference: 493754

Map(s): OS 1:25000 Pathfinder Series No. 762 Worksop South and Staveley

How to get there:

By Public Transport: Daily bus services from Sheffield, Bolsover, Mansfield, Worksop and Chesterfield.

By Car: A616 passes through Clowne. Follow the B6417 in the village. Go over the railway and at the junction near the Anchor, go left to the car park.

The Pub

The Anchor Inn on Mill Street in the middle of Clowne, is a fine old pub. It stands near to the even older market cross. Stones and Mansfield beers are served and the pub also does bar meals every day, plus traditional Sunday lunches. Opening hours are 11.30am – 4pm and 7pm – 11pm Monday to Saturday. Usual Sunday hours. Families are welcome and there's a beer garden. This is one of the pubs where an appearance in designer walking gear will cause a few raised eyebrows.

The Walk

From the car park, walk back along the road to the Anchor and go left, noting the ancient market cross, a reminder of the age of this village. Walk up the road to the junction by the Angel. Cross the main road and bear right along the narrower road past the White Hart. (There's no shortage of pubs in Clowne as you will have realised by now). Note the limestone buildings, a reminder that Clowne sits on the easternmost ridge of Derbyshire limestone. At one time all the buildings here would have been built in the local stone, but now brick predominates. Present day Clowne is basically a large colliery village, but its origins are much older, as the Norman church of St. John Baptist bears witness. Unusually, the church is some way from the present village centre and you don't see it until you are on your way back.

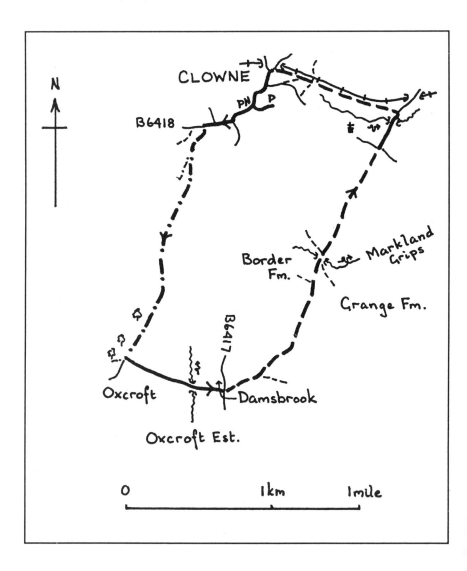

Look Out For 113

Continue along the road until you reach number 113 on the left. Here a narrow alleyway leads between the houses. It is signed as a footpath. When the path reaches the playing fields, go right, along the backs of the terrace until you reach the end. There is a stile on the left, but pause for a moment to admire the view to the right. You are perched on the very edge of the limestone scarp, so the view extends all the way to the Peak District. Even the obvious signs of industry don't seem to mar this expanse. Go through the stile and follow the fence on the left-hand side to the pylon. Continue ahead, with the fence/hedge on your left to reach a gap. Pass through the gap and go straight on, keeping to the right of the solitary tree, by the remains of the hedge. Bear right along the top of the limestone edge to reach a stile by the second pylon. There are good views to the right all along this stretch.

The path continues to hug the edge, with fields to the left and scrub and steep drop to the right. Devotees of sloe gin will find their raw material in abundance here. The next stile is also situated by a pylon. Useful waymarkers are pylons. The path follows a hedge on the left to arrive at another stile to the left of the gate. This takes you out onto a narrow lane, which you cross, going through the gap in the hedge opposite. Now make for the third pylon from the right, straight across the field, to reach a stile in the hedge. Straight on again to a further stile into another little lane. As before, the continuation is immediately opposite, though this time there is a stile in place in the hedge. Still going straight ahead, now make for the left of the second group of buildings. Just before the buildings are reached, there is a gate leading out onto the road. Go left here along the lane, which is narrow and sees very little traffic.

Oxcroft Estate

The map shows this area as Oxcroft Estate, but this is not a housing estate, nor a country estate of the hunting, shooting, fishing variety. It is an area of scattered houses with fields in between and was apparently developed by the government between the two world wars, to encourage small scale market gardening and smallholding for those who were unemployed. While most of the land is still in cultivation, not many of the smallholdings now function as such, though some do. The numbering of the houses is curious too, for irrespective of the name of the road on which they stand, they are numbered in an Oxcroft Estate series.

At Damsbrook cross roads, go over the main road and down the lane marked with the 7.5 tonne weight restriction sign. The lane soon splits three ways, in between two bungalows. Take the middle route, which soon becomes little more than a track. Where the track forks again, the headgear of Cresswell Colliery can be seen to the right. Go left at this point. Whitwell is in view ahead and the chimney of Steetley's quarry can also be seen.

Markland Grips

A track trails in on the left from Border Farm. Interestingly, given the farm name, this track is indeed the parish boundary. A further track trails in from the right, this one coming from Grange Farm. There is an interesting collection of old buses in the field ahead, putting a new slant on the notion of farm diversification. To the right the start of the limestone valley of Markland Grips can be discerned, with some telltale rock outcrops.

The track dips to cross the head of Markland Grips and then again forks. Bear right here, climbing up out of the valley to reach the road. Here bear right and carry on along Hollin Hill Road, ignoring the lane leading off to the right. The road drops quite sharply down to the layby which marks the start of the Clowne Linear Park. The noticeboard at the foot of the steps gives some information about the railway company which built the line which has now become the Linear Park. Unfortunately the artist who drew the pictures has included a drawing of a Great Western Railway locomotive, which is little short of sacrilege.

The Maddest Railway Scheme

The Lancashire Derbyshire and East Coast Railway, who constructed this route, came very late on the railway building scene, in the 1890s. This part of the line was a mere branch from what was a grandiose proposal to link the east coast with the west coast, via the Peak District. The line never got further west than Chesterfield, nor further east than Lincoln, so its title was singularly inaccurate. It was also described as "the maddest scheme ever presented to Parliament" and "the final flowering from the lunatic fringe of railway mania". This section, linking the collieries around Langwith to Sheffield, was one of the saner parts, though even here the closeness of the opposing Midland Railway route makes one wonder whether the capital investment was ever worthwhile.

Go up the steps onto the embankment and follow the course of the old line towards Clowne. The church seen away to the left is St. John Baptist, originally dedicated to All Saints. It was originally built between 1135 and 1154, but was much rebuilt in the more flamboyant Early English and Decorated styles. The age of the church contrasts forcibly with the short life of the railway on which you are now walking.

Carry on along the trail which is pleasantly overgrown. Ignore paths leading off left and right, though if you're a railway enthusiast it is worth deviating to the right at the bridge to see just how close the Midland Railway line is. The former Midland station buildings are soon seen ahead and to the right, but the trail ascends a ramp up to the main road. The LDEC station has vanished as if it had never been. Turn left here, passing the Nags Head and follow the main road round to the Anchor Inn, the chosen pub on this walk. The car park lies just down the road opposite the pub.

9: DALE ABBEY

The Route: Dale Moor – Dale Abbey village – Hermitage – Hermit's Wood – Boyah Grange – Little London – Far Lane – Ockbrook – Hopwellnook –Hopwell School – Constitution Hill – Keys Farm – Sandiacre Lodge – Dale Moor

Distance: 5.4 miles (8.75km)

Start: Lay by on the Dale to Sandiacre road, at the junction with the road to Stanton by Dale. Grid reference: 443384. Public transport users should start at Ockbrook, Ridings Farm

Map(s): OS 1:25000 Pathfinder Series No. 833 Nottingham South West

How to get there:

By Public Transport: Frequent buses to Ockbrook from Derby, except on Sundays. No service to Dale Abbey. Nearest bus route is along the A6096 from Ilkeston to Derby, alighting at Dale Lane End. This service runs Monday to Saturday only.

By Car: A 6096 from Derby or Ilkeston. Dale Abbey is signed from this road. There is very limited parking in the village, so go past the Carpenter's Arms and round the sharp right-hand bend. 500 metres further on you will reach the T-junction. The lay by is on the right.

The Pub

The Carpenter's Arms at Dale Abbey is situated just opposite the junction of the road leading to the hermitage and the village proper. The beer dispensed is Burton Ales. The pub name derives from the original builders and owners, the Hollingworths, who were apparently carpenters by trade. The rear portion of the pub was built first, the front being much more modern. Opening hours are 12noon – 3pm and 7pm – 11pm Monday to Friday, 11am – 3pm and 7pm – 11pm on Saturdays, 12noon – 3pm and 7pm – 10.30pm on Sundays. Food is served daily at lunchtimes and evenings. There is a beer garden for those who can't abide being indoors on a glorious summer day.

The Walk

From the lay by, go over the waymarked stile on the left, heading towards Dale Abbey. Once in the field, bear right, leaving the more obvious track heading straight on. Your footpath is little used, but heads

towards the left of the brick built shed with white windows. You are travelling on the route of an ancient road at this point. The raised strip of ground can be discerned in the field and this leads unerringly to the buildings. On reaching the shed go along the lane on the left. As you round the end of the buildings the great chancel arch of Dale Abbey comes into view ahead.

The path bears right again to reach a gate and stile. In this next field the path continues to follow the old road line, along a prominent embankment. Do not bear left towards the ruins, unless

Chancel arch, Dale Abbey

you are forgoing the pub. The path struggles across a stream, by some thorn bushes and thus reaches a stile. Go diagonally left across this field, which shows no sign of the old road at all, and so reach a stile in the far left-hand corner. This takes you out onto the road. Go left here and walk along the road to the pub.

Dale Abbey

On leaving the pub, cross the main road and go down the lane into the village of Dale Abbey. This is delightful little spot. Almost at the end of the village "main" street there is a triangular junction and a map of the area. Bear left here. The Manor House is on the left and between the buildings you catch the occasional glimpse of the ruined arch of the abbey. A footpath on the left leads to the abbey ruins. These are worth a look. The abbey of St Mary was built in the 12th and 13th centuries and

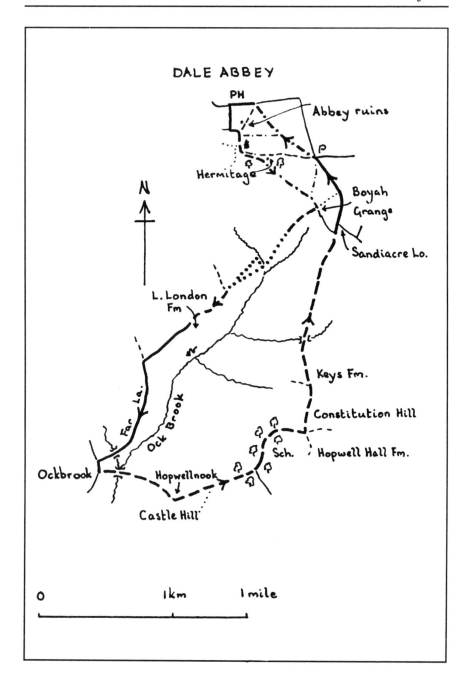

DALE ABBEY

PH

Abbey ruins

P

Hermitage

Boyah Grange

Sandiacre Lo.

N

L. London Fm

Keys Fm.

Constitution Hill

Far La.

Ock Brook

Sch.

Hopwell Hall Fm.

Ockbrook

Hopwellnook

Castle Hill

0   1km   1 mile

belonged to the Premonstratensian order. It was dissolved in 1538 as part of the general Dissolution of the Monasteries ordered by Henry VIII. Only the great chancel arch now stands, but the outlines of other buildings can be made out in the surrounding fields. Local legend has it that the stone from the abbey was plundered by the villagers, but that the arch was retained because there had long been an agreement that no tithe was payable while the arch stood. Having looked at the ruins, return to the lane to continue the walk. Continue along the lane to reach a waymarked gate.

All Saints Church

All Saints Church lies just ahead and a curious place it is, part farmhouse, part church. It is one of the tiniest churches in England, only taking on its religious function when its greater neighbour, the abbey, was destroyed in the Reformation. The church is in one of the former outhouses to the abbey, probably the Infirmary. The building dates from the 12th century and was originally thatched. The farmhouse to which the church is attached was a pub at one time, called The Bluebell. To complete the picture it has to be said that there was a connecting door between the pub and the church! Legend has it that Robin Hood came here to attend the wedding of his fellow outlaw Alan a Dale. However, the dates don't fit at all, but who cares? The church proper only measures 26 feet x 25 feet, but to make up for its tininess, it boasts one of the largest chalices in the country, measuring 9 inches high by 15 inches in diameter. The church contains a balcony, which can only be reached from a flight of precarious steps up the outside of the building. Inside, the layout is also unusual in that the pulpit, reading desk and clerk's pew are behind the altar. There are also some fine mediaeval wall paintings. Well worth a visit, but unfortunately you can no longer use the church as a local version of Gretna Green; this privilege having been withdrawn in 1754.

Go straight on through the farmyard gate, ignoring the stile on the right. The path now begins to climb and there are views across the village to the abbey ruins and the windmill on the opposite hilltop. A gate leads into Hermits Wood and a prominent track carries on through the wood, but this is not your route. Instead, look out for a flight of steps on the right. These lead unerringly up to a higher path, from which a short path drops down left, to the Hermit's Cave. This is a strange carved rock structure set into the hillside with good views over the abbey to the windmill on the opposite hillside. This part of the walk is very popular, but you will soon lose the crowds. The tale about the Hermitage tells of a Derby baker, one Cornelius, who received a vision in 1130-40 and was directed to this spot to spend the rest of his life in prayer. The hermitage itself is part natural cave, part man made. The windmill of course is much younger. It is a post mill, where the whole superstructure, weighing about 50 tonnes, turns round a central post. It is now fully restored.

Retrace your steps back onto the higher path and here turn left, passing over the top of the cave. Continue on this narrow path through the wood, keeping close company with the fence and hedge on the right. Ignore other paths leading off into the wood and keep on the top side of the trees until you reach a stile on the right. This gives out into fields.

In the field, bear left, heading towards the pylon and the piece of fencing in the hedge opposite. This proves to be a stile. In the next field go diagonally across. Keep to the left of the pylon in mid field. Continue ahead to reach a stile in the fence, to the right of the big tree. There is an extensive view left, including the water tower at Swingate, which owners of the Nottinghamshire Pub Walks book will remember.

The Old Road to Boyah Grange

Boyah Grange can be seen ahead and there is a curious elongated depression in the ground leading towards the buildings. This is probably another old road. The footpath closely follows the depression and thus reaches a stile. At this point you enter the farmyard. The walk was originally intended to bear left at this point, to pass between the farm buildings and reach the lane just beyond. However, a gate across this route proclaims that the way through the farm to the lane is private, and as it is not marked on the definitive map as a footpath or bridleway, the route is effectively barred. The presence of the old road in the field leads the author to suspect that the original route did indeed pass through the farm yard.

Instead of worrying about the rights and wrongs of the route through Boyah Grange, negotiate the stile and bear right, skirting the buildings to reach a gateway. This leads onto a rough lane. Follow the track until it turns sharp right, heading for Malthouse Farm. At this point a footpath continues straight ahead, through a stile. This is your route. The OS map now shows a path bearing right across the field towards the kink in the far hedge. You can rest assured that this does not exist. Instead, keep to the remains of the left-hand boundary of the field, on the same alignment as the lane you have just left. In this manner you will reach a stile in the far hedge, close to the stream.

In the next field there is a temptation to continue alongside the brook, but the path seems to bear right instead. Cut diagonally across the field towards the white notice on the big tree. If there are crops growing in this field, it may prove easier to go right at the stile and the left at the hedge corner. This would have the merit of returning you more quickly to the line of the path as shown on the map. Either way you will eventually come to the white notice. The inscription on the notice board is a laugh. Locko Park Estates ask you to keep to the path! Would that it were so simple.

London to Scotland in Record Time

Keep alongside the hedge to reach a narrow, muddy lane. Ahead is Little London Farm, part of which is timber-framed. Beyond the farm the track becomes a proper tarred road, but sees very little traffic. You drop gently towards Ockbrook and there is an extensive view to the south. Continue down Far Lane, passing Scotland Farm on the left, surely one of the quickest walks between London and Scotland on record.

The give-away green metal gates of the Derwent Aqueduct are passed and then the lane crosses the stream on a bridge. Ahead lie the first houses of Ockbrook. Turn left at the main road and then, in about 100 metres, go left again at the footpath sign, just before the house with the curved wall and the shuttered windows.

A Grand View over the Trent Valley

Despite the footpath sign, this is again a tarred lane. You cross a cattle-grid and the Ock Brook, before being greeted by a monstrosity of a modern farm building on the left. The track climbs steadily up Castle Hill and for each foot of height gained the view becomes better. Eventually at Hopwellnook House, there is an enormous view over the Trent Valley. There are the inevitable power stations, but the eye is drawn more towards the blue line of hills that denote Charnwood Forest, and to the tower of Breedon on the Hill church.

You don't see much of Ockbrook on this walk, but the village was originally a Saxon settlement. It has now been engulfed by modern housing, but still boasts a much "restored" Norman church and the fascinating 18th century Moravian settlement.

The path skirts round to the right of Hopwellnook House, turns left and continues to climb towards the trees on the summit of the hill. On the right are the twin green domes covering the valves on the aqueduct. When the track meets the trees, there is a waymarked stile by the gate and a sign proclaiming that this is Hopwell School. It is worth pausing here for a moment to admire the view, which is even more extensive than it was at Hopwellnook House. The hills of Cannock Chase can be distinguished to the south west, as well as the various places mentioned earlier.

Go over the stile and continue up the track until it joins the main driveway to the school. Follow the footpath signs up the drive until you reach the first buildings where there is a road sign warning you to slow down because of speed bumps. Unless you are an incredibly fast walker, or you are doing this walk on roller skates, the sign need not concern you, except that there is also a footpath sign at this point, directing you to the left. Leave the drive and follow the waymarked path past the rose bushes and into the wood which fringes the school. Various paths cross or join your route, but the public footpath is always waymarked. Skirt round the northern side of the school to reach a stile at the edge of the wood. Here you enter fields again.

Venison on The Hoof

Follow the track up towards Hopwell Hall Farm, seen a little way ahead. Just by the farm there is a crossing of tracks and paths. A rough waymarked track goes straight ahead, but your route lies to the left, over Constitution Hill, following the power line. As the path begins to descend you will be surprised to see what look like red deer in the fields ahead. Closer acquaintance confirms the initial suspicion, for this is a deer farm and there are many of these magnificent animals grazing in the fields. The broad track passes Keys Farm and continues to descend to reach a culverted stream in the bottom of the dip. Here there is a gate and the track enters open fields again.

The path has obviously been a narrow lane at some time in the past as there are the remains of boundaries on either side. Go straight on, up the field to reach a waymarked gate. This leads into a tightly fenced and hedged lane, which is very muddy. Sharing this confined space with the homeward bound herd of cows, as the author did when testing this walk, is an interesting experience. The lane continues for some distance, though there are various gateways on the left for the cattle to use, leaving the way ahead clear. Eventually you reach a gate and stile. The lane then joins a tarred road coming in from the left. The buildings on the left look vaguely familiar, which is not surprising as this is the other side of Boyah Grange which you past on the outward trip.

Continue ahead along the lane to reach the "main" road at the T-junction. There is no footway alongside this road, but fortunately there is a verge. Follow the main road past the pond. The road now bends to the left and begins to descend in a cutting. Here there is neither footway nor verge, so take care and keep into the side. You soon emerge from the cutting and there, just in front is the lay-by where those of you who insist on using cars should find their vehicle.

The Carpenter's Arms, Dale Abbey

10: DOVERIDGE

The Route: Doveridge Church – Dove Suspension Bridge – Dove Bridge –Sidford Wood – Eaton Hall Lane – Cavendish Arms – Doveridge Church

Distance: 3.25 miles (5.25km)

Start: Doveridge Church, Grid reference: 114341

Map(s): OS 1:25000 Pathfinder Series No. 831 Uttoxeter

How to get there:

By Public Transport: Daily bus service from Uttoxeter and Burton. Saturdays only service from the Potteries.

By Car: A50 from Derby or the Potteries. Doveridge is signed near the Cavendish Arms. It is an awkward junction, particularly when joining the main road. Go down the lane by the pub, to the cross roads by the well, then right, to the church.

The Pub

The Cavendish Arms, Doveridge, takes its name from the local landowners, who were relatives of the Dukes of Devonshire of Chatsworth. The one drawback to this otherwise excellent pub is its proximity to the busy A50 road. Despite this there is an outdoor seating area. However, the village is soon to be by-passed, so peace should be restored. The landlord is a member of the Guild of Master Cellarmen, so you would expect a decent pint of ale. Nor will you be disappointed. There is a choice of Tetleys, Marstons and Burton beers available. Opening hours are 11.30am – 3pm and 6pm – 11pm Monday to Saturday, 12noon – 3pm and 7pm – 10.30pm on Sundays. Food is served seven days a week at lunchtimes and evenings.

The Walk

Doveridge village proper stands back from the A50. It is a pleasant spot with some interesting historical features. There are a number of 18th century buildings in the village and a timber framed Old Hall. St Cuthbert's Church is worth a look round, either before you set out on the walk or after you get back. The church is mentioned in Domesday Book and the present building has 12th and 13th century portions. The yew tree in the churchyard is reputed to be 1000 years old. Local legend has it that Robin Hood married Maid Marion here. A much travelled man was our Robin! However, this area was once forested and Loxley Hall, (he was Robin of Loxley you will remember), still stands, less than five miles away. So much for the claims of Nottingham and Sherwood!

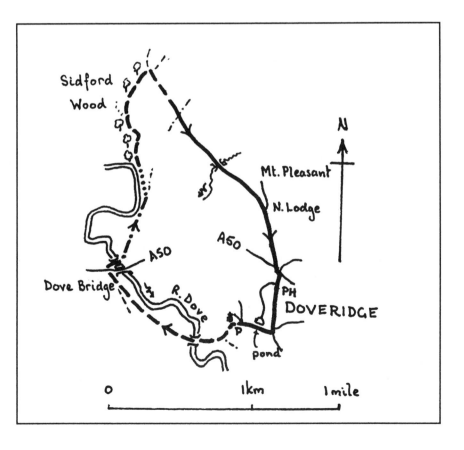

Suspended Over the Dove

Go down the lane to the left of the church. This was once the old route to the Doveridge Mill, now sadly demolished. As you descend the lane, the glint of water can be seen ahead through the trees. At the bottom of the hill the lane goes right and there are two footpaths going off on the left. Your route lies along the second of these, which turns out to be a fine raised causeway, tightly fenced from the surrounding fields. A footbridge is crossed over one of the many drainage streams on this low lying and flat land. Ahead you can see the spire of Uttoxeter church and the unusual suspension bridge which carries the path over the Dove.

Normally the crossing of the River Dove would land you in Staffordshire, but not in this instance. You continue from the bridge along a flood bank, raised up above the surrounding meadows. There are a couple of gun emplacements on the left here The locals swear this was installed to prevent German invasion and not to stop an incursion from Uttoxeter. The track bears right, following the river at a discreet distance. Eventually another drainage channel is crossed. This is the county boundary and you now enter Staffordshire. The boundary actually follows the old course of the River Dove. Over the years the river has shifted due to flooding or deliberate diversion, but not so the county boundary. This preserves the old river route, even though the result is a geographical nonsense. As you near the A50, there is another gun emplacement on the right and then you reach a stile. This takes you onto a field track which leads up onto the main road.

Cross the A50 with great care. It is a fast and busy road. Go over the stile opposite, having admired the old bridge from the relative safety of the footway. A scramble through scrubby bushes leads onto the remains of the old road. Here turn right onto the old bridge. The original medieval bridge was widened and rebuilt in 1691 as the plaque proclaims. As a piece of architecture it is infinitely preferable to its modern successor, but the noise of modern motor traffic prevents any real appreciation of the bridge or the river at this point.

Back into Derbyshire

At the far end of the bridge you re-enter Derbyshire. Bear left down the slope by the paling fence to reach a stile. This takes you out onto the meadows again. A glance at the map will show that the county boundary runs up the middle of this field, even though the river is away to the left. The path is not very obvious underfoot in these fields. Bear right, heading towards the dead tree, seen on the bank-side ahead. This route cuts off the bend in the river and soon gives fine views of the rocky outcrops which plunge steeply to the water's edge. An unusual feature, looking quite out of place in this otherwise gentle landscape.

Good View Over the Dove

Soon a stile is reached, just to the left of the gateway and the riverbank is rejoined. Here the path forks and it is very easy to go wrong. Do not follow the hedge on the right, but go straight up the nose of the hill. There is a good view over Uttoxeter from the top. Trees fringe the cliffs on the left and fortunately prevent any serious attempts at exploration. Keep alongside the trees on your left. A hedge soon joins from the right, making a broad green lane. The path becomes increasingly muddy, hemmed in on the left by the trees and on the right by a hedge, which draws ever closer to the trees until you are walking in a virtual tunnel of branches. The muddiness is not helped by the presence of cattle. Eventually at the end of the "lane", you will reach a gateway, but the path actually descends to the left. There is a signpost, cunningly hidden in the trees. Keep the fence to your right and the stream to your left and thus reach a stile on the right. This takes you out into open fields again. The path now skirts the left-hand edge of the field with Sidford Wood dropping steeply away on the left and farmland to the right. Head for the white sign board ahead.

The map shows a path leading off to the left, but there is no sign of it in practice. It would be difficult to traverse the steep wooded slope in any case. On reaching the white sign board, you are informed that you are on the Staffordshire Way, here making a brief incursion into Derbyshire. Bear right here, across the end of the field to a further white board. Here you join a track and go right. The route is signed as a bridleway to Doveridge, but at the gate and cattle-grid at the end of the field it becomes a narrow, tarred lane. The rest of the walk needs little description, for you remain on the lane all the way back to the junction with the A50, opposite the Cavendish Arms. Despite the route being on a tarred road, it is very pleasant. There is very little traffic and the hedgerows are full of wildflowers, bird and animal life, one particularly attractive spot being where the stream comes under the lane and there is a brick built trough. There are occasional good views to the right, over towards Uttoxeter and the Dove Valley. The lane from Upwoods Farm is joined near North Lodge. The peace and tranquillity of this spot are soon to be disrupted by the construction of the Doveridge By-pass. The lane is to be carried over the new road on a bridge, so at least you'll not have to worry about crossing a fast and busy dual carriageway.

Back to Doveridge

Eventually the first houses of Doveridge are reached and soon after the lane emerges onto the A50. Cross with care to reach the pub, then, having drunk your fill, either catch the bus or proceed into the village, turning right by the well. The well was one of a number in the village, but it is now capped and surrounded with a garden and a seat. Finish your walk by strolling along Lakeside, to reach the church and your car.

11: HEAGE

The Route: Heage Tavern – Sawmills – Wingfield Park Farm – Lodge Hill Farm – Wingfield Park – Pentrich Mill – Pentrich Church – Fields Farm – Lr. Hartshay – Starvehimvalley Bridge – Bond Lane Farm – Heage Tavern

Distance: 6.25 miles (9.75 km). Allow 3.5 hours with a stop at Pentrich church

Start: Heage Tavern, Grid reference: 373505

Map(s): OS 1:25000 Pathfinder Series No. 794, Crich and Bullbridge

How to get there:

By Public Transport: Monday to Saturday services to Heage from Derby, Belper and Ripley.

By Car: A610 to Buckland Hollow, (very awkward junction), then follow B6013 to Heage. Left along B6374 to Heage Tavern, 250 –300 metres. Parking on the Ripley Road just beyond the pub.

The Pub

The Heage Tavern, a free house in the centre of the village, is perfectly situated for this walk. It is a friendly pleasant pub with a good range of beers on hand-pump, including Marstons Pedigree, Ind Coope, Tetley and Burton Bitters and Ansells Mild. There's also a guest beer each week. For the cider drinker there's Addelstones' cider on draught as well. Food is available throughout opening hours, which are 12noon – 11pm Monday to Friday, 11am – 11pm on Saturdays, 12noon – 3pm and 7pm – 10.30pm on Sundays. There's a large bar area, split to form two smaller "rooms" and there are tables outside on the Ripley Road, though these can be noisy when the road is busy.

The Walk

From the front door of the pub, go right, along the main road, heading uphill to the cross roads by the White Hart. This is another grand pub, serving Bass beers. At the cross roads, go straight on, along School Lane, which is signed to Nether Heage and Ambergate.

Heage has no particularly obvious centre. The area became industrial in the 18th century with the opening of coal mines and iron foundries, utilising the nearby Cromford Canal. The name Heage derives from the Anglo Saxon "Heagge", meaning a high place. The church is dedicated to St. Luke and was a timber structure until 1661 when it was rebuilt in stone following a storm. It has an unusual octagonal shaped bell tower.

Almost at the brow of the hill, there is a footpath sign on the right, directing you to Sawmills and Ladygrove. Go through the stile along a narrow "ginnel" by the stables. Another stile leads you into open fields and there is a view left, to the restored Heage windmill.

I Spy Crich

There is an imperceptible crossing of paths at this stile. Your route officially lies diagonally left across the field, but the walked path heads for the prominent oak tree straight ahead. On reaching the oak, the path turns left to run alongside the hedge, until it reaches a stile in the corner of the field. There is a good view from here over Ambergate to Crich.

Go through this stile into the field. The next stile is in the opposite fence and hedge, about 50 metres down the hillside, hidden by a hawthorn. Once you have located and negotiated this stile, the path heads across the next field to the gap between the trees and the grass covered bank on the right. The path joins a prominent terraced track, coming up from Heage Hall, seen to the left. However, the obviousness of this track is a trap for the unwary, for, as the patch of gorse is reached, an indistinct path diverges left, to a well hidden stile in the hawthorn hedge. Heage Hall was once in the ownership of the Pole family. Parts of the house are 15th century and both the hall and these nearby fields are reputedly haunted by the ghosts of a couple of 18th century inhabitants, George Pole and his wife.

Derwent Aqueduct

Having located both path and stile, and entered new pastures, bear right to pass between two trees, some 25 metres down what remains of the opposite hedge. Go across the next field to a stile to the left of the metal gate. The following field houses a green steel domed structure. This is one of the many inspection hatches to the Derwent Aqueduct. The

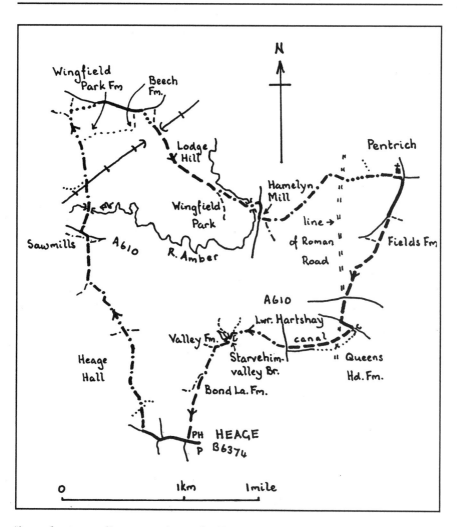

Aqueduct supplies water from the Derwent Dams in the Peak District, to the cities of Derby, Nottingham and Leicester. Go to the left of this structure and, keeping on the same alignment as in the previous field, head for a stile in the middle of the hedge. Still keeping to the same alignment, head for the left-hand corner of the field, to a stile to the left of a solitary stone post.

Go through the stile and then diagonally right to the corner, where there is another stile to the right of the gap. This takes you into a lovely old fashioned hay meadow. The path continues alongside the wall on the left, very soon reaching a stile by a gate. Go through the stile and then diagonally right to the far corner where there is a gateway. At this point a track is joined and is followed, with the wall on your left. Crich Church and Stand are in view ahead.

Keep straight on along the track, with the wall cum hedge on your left, to a stile in the corner of the field by the ash tree. Continue ahead into a narrow lane, noting the curious practice of putting old farm machinery out to grass as if it were a redundant cart horse.

The lane soon passes in front of the farm house and straight ahead there is a stile to the left of the white gate. This takes you onto a wide bridge which once spanned the Ambergate to Pye Bridge railway and the Cromford canal. The railway site is now in use by a road transport firm and their landscaping efforts do them great credit.

The Origin of Ambergate

The lane swings right towards the A610, but go left here instead, down a steep flight of steps to the road. At the main road, go left along the footway. Cross the road with care and very soon go right, through a waymarked stile by a gate. This takes you down by the side of the playing fields into open pasture again. The way ahead now lies across the River Amber, using the footbridge to the left of the pipe. The river gives its name to the nearby village of Ambergate, the "gate" element of the name being indicative of an ancient route. In this case it is most apt, for the valley of the Amber is the only significant gap in the hills that line the east bank of the Derwent. As such it has always been a focus of transport routes.

The path on the far side of the river is paved for a short way. It follows the hedge on the right to the right-hand corner of the field, where there is a gap. Do not go through the gap, but seek out the stile in the scrub covered fence ahead. The fence guards the railway line.

No Dithering on The Railway Line!

No country branch line this, so do not dither on the crossing, but walk over as quickly as possible, (having checked there are no trains coming of course). This is the Derby – Sheffield main line with trains passing regularly at speeds in excess of 70mph. A quick glance to the right as you cross, reveals a surprising view straight through Wingfield Tunnel!

Go over the stile on the far side of the railway and follow the hedge on the right, up towards Wingfield Park Farm. Continue upwards, through a stile by the gate, until the farm is reached. The map shows a path to the right at this point, through the farm buildings. It does not exist, so continue up the field past the farm, to another stile. The path continues through a series of fields, always keeping to the right-hand side and passing through gateways. Eventually you will spot a stile diagonally left, but ignore this. Keep on along the right-hand edge of the field to the next gateway and then go right. There is a well hidden and defended stile at this point, half buried in a holly bush.

Having extricated yourself from the holly, there is a choice of paths. Your route lies straight on, across the middle of the field, heading towards the pole and the solitary tree. If your navigation, and these instructions, are correct, you should find a stile in the middle of the holly hedge, just to the right of the holly tree.

In the next field bear left and head for a stile just to the left of the white gate, which is the entrance to Wingfield Park Farm. The farm itself is seen to the right. At the white gate, turn right, along the road. There is no footway and hardly any verge either, but fortunately there is not a lot of traffic. There is a good view back towards Heage from this point.

Pass the entrance to Mount Pleasant Farm on the right, noting the lovely hay meadows, packed with flowers in the Spring. Then, a little over 100 metres past the entrance to Beech Hill Farm, there is a stile on the right, opposite the black gate. The stile is easily missed and even when you've found it and got over it you'll find little semblance of a path. The route lies across the field, to a stile and gate to the left of the electricity pole. There is a view across to Swanwick from here, but don't try and admire it from the stile as it is very rickety.

Standing on Top of the Tunnel

The next stile lies ahead and to the left, across another hay meadow, in a newly mortared piece of wall. This takes you onto the access drive to Lodge Hill Farm. Here go right, to the stile on the left of the white gate. You are now standing on the top of Wingfield Tunnel, which must be very shallow at this point.

Follow the lane up through a cutting towards the farm. Pass a walled orchard on the left, then go straight on, past the cattle shed. Beyond the farm, bear left down the track, with a fence and hedge on the left, until a gateway is reached at the bottom of the field. The track goes through the gateway and bears right by the wall of Wingfield Park. While this route is temptingly obvious, it is not the way you want. Your path lies to the left just beyond the gateway, down to the trees that fringe the Amber. Here there is a sketchy path along the riverside, and this you now follow, avoiding the nettles as best you can.

The path swings left at a loop in the river, to reach a concrete bridge. Beyond the bridge the path slopes up to join the road, where you go right.

Pentrich Or Hamlyn Mill?

Cross the road near Hamlyn Mill. This is also known as Pentrich Mill and is signposted as such in Pentrich village. The present structure was built in 1878, though there was probably an earlier building on the site. Just opposite the mill, go left, up a footpath signed to Pentrich. The path goes up a narrow enclosed way until a stile is reached.

Once over the stile, the path forks. Keep straight on, up the field with the hawthorn hedge on your right. Follow the hedge as it bears round to the left and reaches a stile in the top corner of the field. Negotiate the stile and continue straight on, still following the hedge on your right, to reach a waymarked gateway, again on the right. Go through the gateway, with the hedge now on your left and pass under the power line. Keep on the left-hand side of the field to the far end, where there is a gap in the hedge. Through the gap and into another field. Pentrich village is now in view ahead.

Head across the field to the unseen exit stile, which lies to the left of the prominent oak tree and to the right of the new stone house. The path is in fact heading direct to the church, but this is obscured by trees. Part way across the field you cross the line of the Roman Road, the Ryknield Street, but only the most practised eye would notice it. Just to the north of Pentrich was a small Roman fort and the road then headed for Chesterfield and Templeborough (Rotherham). Southwards, the road was heading for the fort at Derventio (Derby).

Pentrich, an Ill Fated Rebellion

Having missed the Roman Road, but found the exit stile, go over it and proceed up the middle of the next field to a stile in the top right-hand corner. This takes you into the churchyard. Your route takes you along the tarmac path on the right-hand side of the churchyard, to a flight of steps that descend to the road. However, it is a pity to pass the church without a look inside. The church is dedicated to St. Matthew. It has some fine Norman stone work dating back to the founding of the church in the 1150s. Five Saxon crosses have been identified in use as lintels for the church windows! The font is inscribed as 1662, but it is thought that the bowl itself is Norman. It was restored to its position in the 19th century, having been used as a bath for salting beef for many years! The church also has unusual tiered seating. The manor of Pentrich was given to the church in 1152 and it stayed in church hands until Henry VIII's time. The Cavendish family then held the manor until 1950.

In the churchyard there are a number of seats, where you can muse on the fact that this small village has its name engraved in British social history as being the nerve centre of the ill fated Pentrich rebellion of 1817. The strands of the revolt are complex, based on rising prices, depression in local industry and agriculture, fear of new machinery and so on. Led by Jeremiah Brandreth, the men of Pentrich and their neighbours in South Wingfield, marched on Nottingham. The rising was a disaster and at Kimberley, near Nottingham, the "rebels" fled at the first sign of resistance. The ringleaders were tried for high treason and Brandreth and two others executed on 7th November 1817. Of more pleasant memory is the Damson Social, a mass collecting of damsons, which use to take place in September, coinciding with the church patronal festival. The damsons were collected for dye, not eating.

Leaving the churchyard, descend to the road by the steps mentioned earlier and go right. Pass the Dog Inn, serving Bass Beers and at the edge of the village, bear left along a road marked with a No Through Road sign. This was the main road into Pentrich before the present B6016 was built. Beyond the stile by the gate the lane becomes a classic hollow-way. The track passes Fields Farm and soon after, there is a view left over to Ripley and Butterley. Soon you will notice a stile to the right, but ignore this and carry on down the lane.

The lane ends abruptly at two gates. The footpath continues from a stile between the two gates and runs tightly hemmed in by fences and a superabundance of nettles. This is not shown on the OS map. The narrow way soon emerges onto a paved path, which descends steeply to the "improved" A610. Cross the main road with care to the bus stop opposite and seek out the path to the right of the shelter. This leaves the main road behind and runs as a tarmac path, across the field to the old A610 in Lower Hartshay. The original settlement here sat at the cross roads between the Ryknield Street and the Ambergate Ripley route. The name Hartshay derives from "hart", the old English word for deer. This area and the nearby Buckland, were once part of a royal hunting forest.

Go left here along the road, until the bridge over the Cromford Canal is
reached near the Gate Inn. The map shows paths on either side of the
canal, but you go through the stile on the right just before the bridge.
This leads onto the towpath alongside the canal. There is water in the
canal at this point despite it having been abandoned for many years. Of
the alleged path on the opposite side of the cut, there is little or no sign,
the way being blocked by pig pens and guinea fowl hutches.

Along the Cromford Canal

The canal was built in the late 18th century and brought a new
prosperity to the area based on coal and iron, though at a considerable
cost in terms of environmental damage. After walking a short distance
along the towpath, the remains of a narrow boat in the last stages of
disintegration will be seen, and soon afterwards the canal itself vanishes,
having been infilled. The towpath continues however. Keep alongside
the fence on the right, through Lower Hartshay, until a road is reached,
crossing the former canal. Go over the road and keep straight on,
between the houses on the right and the "canal" on the left, to a stile
which takes you out onto the "towpath" again. The canal is completely
infilled at this point, but the path is clear enough, alongside the hedge.
Eventually the narrow, hedged strip widens out and all evidence of the
canal is lost, except for the path, which heads across the field to a stile in
the middle of the barbed wire fence. There is a cunningly concealed
ditch here as well as the fence. Negotiate both and head across the next
field, towards the white house.

As you near the white house, bear left, keeping the fence to your right. A
stile returns you to the towpath again at a delightfully preserved piece of
canal, well kept and still in water. There is a lovely little bridge over the
canal and your route lies over this. It is reached by diverging right, just
before the bridge, then going left on reaching the track. The bridge
rejoices in the odd and ominous name of Starvehimvalley Bridge. From
the bridge you can see that what was once a winding hole for turning
boats has been cleared out to make a fishing pond. Once over the bridge,
bear right and cross the inlet pipe, which keeps this part of the canal in
water, to reach a stile by a gate. Negotiate the stile and follow the track
to the right towards Valley Farm – not to the left through another gate.
Keep ahead through another gate, then just before the farm, leave the
track and bear left, up the field keeping the hedge on your left. The path
is not at all obvious here, but the hedge is a sure guide and at the top of
the field you should reach a stile alongside a gate.

Go through the stile into a narrow and overgrown lane, pausing to look back over the valley to Lower Hartshay and Pentrich. Follow the lane, noting the green metal gates on either side which mark the course of the Derwent Aqueduct, and passing Bond Lane Farm. Heage now comes into view ahead. The lane continues, with Bowmer and Kirkland's plant yard on the right, to emerge as Bond Lane, onto the main road, right alongside the Heage Tavern.

Starvehimvalley Bridge

12: HOLYMOORSIDE

The Route: Holymoorside – Milldam – Woodside Farm – Gladwins Wood – Stone Edge Golf Course – Stone Edge – Stone Edge Farm – Stubbing Great Pond – Harper Hill – Broadgorse Farm – Walton Lodge Farm – Pine Lodge – Holymoorside

Distance: 5.75 miles (9.25km). Allow 2 to 3 hours, excluding pub visit

Start: Layby near The Alders, opposite the Bulls Head. Grid reference: 339693

Map(s): OS 1:25000 Pathfinder Series No. 761, Chesterfield

How to get there:

By Public Transport: Daily service from Chesterfield. From the bus stop by the Village Hall in the Square, walk down the hill to the Bulls Head and turn left.

By Car: A619 from Chesterfield or Baslow. Holymoorside is signed from Chanderhill. Go into the village, keeping left at the Square, then turning left by the Bulls Head.

The Pub

The Bulls Head is a grand village local, serving John Smiths, Boddington's, and a guest beer. There are tables and seats outside for walkers with sandwiches, but the pub serves meals at lunchtimes except Sundays. Opening hours are 12noon – 3.30pm Monday to Saturday, 12noon – 3pm and 7pm –10.30pm on Sundays. The pub was originally a farmhouse, first opening its doors to public drinking in 1881, an early example of farm diversification! There are old photos of the village on the walls and despite its proximity to Chesterfield, Holymoorside has retained a village atmosphere which is well portrayed in this pub.

The Walk

Holymoorside retains its village feel, even though it has grown considerably in recent years because of its proximity to Chesterfield. The name is supposed to relate to the moorland surrounding Harewood Grange, which used to be in the ownership of Beauchief Abbey. However, this derivation seems unlikely and the name is more probably from the Anglo Saxon words meaning a clearing on the hillside. Although the village is now mainly given over to commuter housing and agriculture, it was until the early part of this century involved in mining, quarrying and cotton manufacturing. The oldest building is probably Hipper Hall, dating from the 16th century. From the Bulls Head, go left, past the lay-by in front of The Alders, and up the road to the United Reform Church on the right. Just beyond the church, go right along a track between stone gate posts. There is no footpath sign. At the end of the track, there is a waymarked stile by the white gates. The path continues with views to the right over the mill dam.

Where the path forks, bear left to a stile which leads into the wood. Ignore the Private signs and paths leading off to the left, keeping instead to the lower edge of the wood. A path joins from the left and at this point your path bears right. The way dips to cross a stream on a stone slab bridge before emerging into fields. Head towards the farm on a non too distinct path. Nearing the farm a track is joined and here go right instead of going into the farmyard. The track soon leads through a gateway into another field. Go left at the distinct crossing of tracks and ascend to a stile by the side of a gate. Your route now lies along a rough walled lane, with Gladwins Wood on the right and open fields to the left.

The lane climbs steadily, with widening views to the left over the dam and Holymoorside. The lane is quite wide and the main track often muddy. At the worst places, walkers have beaten alternative paths.

Eventually, at the top of the fields, a gateway is reached and the track enters the wood. Immediately ahead is another gate, but don't go through it, your path leads up to the right alongside the wall.

The path rises steadily through the wood, with many twists and turns. There is some evidence of a broader hollow way on the right, which passes through a holly tunnel at one point. Mostly however, the path walked is narrow and muddy, but distinct.

The Wild Wood and The Golf Course

This is no manicured woodland, but one which has been left alone for many years. In Spring it is alive with bird song and wild flowers; and infested with large black wood ants. As the path levels out it comes

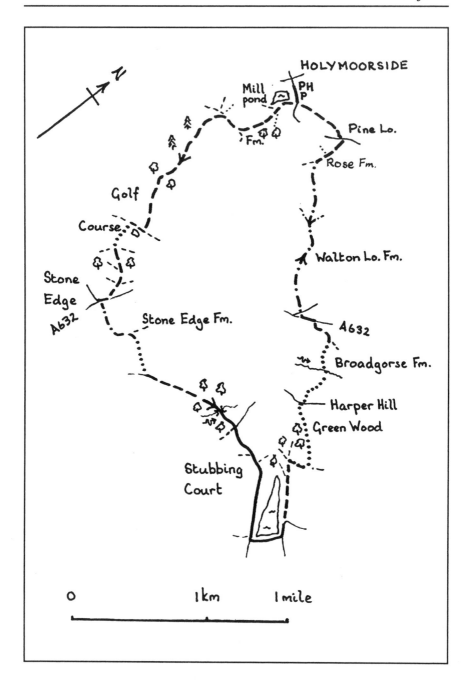

alongside an apparently isolated golf tee, part of Stone Edge Golf Course, but a further short length of woodland walking leads you out on to the main course. Here a notice suggests you turn left and follow the edge of the golf links up to the pond. This is sound advice, although the current edition of the Pathfinder map shows the path going across the fairway to the farmhouse. Discretion being the better part of valour, go left and skirt the edge of the course and the wood. Pass a tattered yellow flag which serves as a waymark, to reach a track by the pond.

There is a signpost here, and you go right, checking first to see if anyone is about to play a shot from the tee on the hillside above the pond. If not, go along the track past the pond to the farmhouse. Ignoring the footpath sign pointing left, follow the track through the gate, along the front of the buildings to the white direction sign and stile on the left. Go over the stile and head up through the "rough", onto the fairway, heading for a post and sapling ahead. Keep a sharp look-out for flying golf balls. The tee is to your right and the green to your left, so you should be safe from attack from one side at least!

When the sapling and post are reached, you will see a white sign board ahead, at the edge of the wood. This is your route, straight across the fairway. At the sign it is safe to pause and admire the view over Chesterfield, before negotiating the stile and entering the wood.

Stone Edge Plantation and A Grand View

Ignore paths to the right and left and go straight into the wood. Stone Edge Plantation is a delightful mixed woodland. Its only drawback is its regular use for motor cycle scrambling, which tends to create a multitude of tracks as well as being noisy. Still, there is no route finding problem. At each junction of tracks, carry straight on until the main A632 road is reached at a gateway. As you approach the road, you will notice piles of stone, half hidden by the trees. All this area was worked for gritstone in the last century and these are the spoil heaps.

At the main road go right, keeping on the verge, (there's no footway), up towards the road junction at the brow of the hill. You will see a footpath sign on the opposite side of the road. Cross the A632 with care to reach the sign and stile. This is a magnificent viewpoint, one of the finest in the area, with a vista over the whole of eastern Derbyshire to Nottinghamshire and the Trent Valley. If local legend is to be believed you can see as far as Lincoln Cathedral, but not, I suspect, without binoculars.

Nestling directly below in the valley is Stubbing Court and its Pond, while behind you is the Pinnacle Rock, the highest point on Stone Edge.

Go over the stile and descend the path towards Stubbing, with the wall on your left. This first stretch appears to go through the edge of a garden, but it is a right of way. Another stile takes you into open fields. Continue down beside the wall to a further stile into an overgrown lane. Turn left along the lane, heading for Stone Edge Farm. Just before the farm, there is a stile in the wall on the right. Go over this stile and cut across the corner of the field to the sign post by the gateway. Go through the gate and alongside the barn, before turning right through another gate, passing a more modern barn on your left. Follow the wall down, keeping it on your left, ignoring inviting looking gateways, until you reach the bottom of the field.

On the Hazards of Chicken Farms

As you approach the stream at the bottom of the field, a peculiar smell begins to assail the nostrils. It comes from the chicken farm ahead and not, thank goodness, from the stream. The brook is easily crossed by a farm bridge after negotiating a stile. The way ahead lies up the far bank, with one group of chicken huts on your left. At the farm track, there is a signpost. Go left here and bid a hasty goodbye to the chicken farm.

Continue down the farm track, which soon joins the drive from Nether House Farm and becomes a tarred road. Carry on down the lane, with Harehill Plantation and the stream on your left.

Stubbing Court Ponds, a Favourite with Birdwatchers

The stream is crossed on a little stone bridge and then a short distance further on there is a slippery ford. This is best avoided by using the pedestrian bridge on the left. A little way beyond the ford there is a road junction and the back entrance to Stubbing Court.

Keep straight on at the road junction. The wall on the right encloses the parkland of Stubbing Court. The house can just be seen but there is a better view further on. The area of trees on your left, in the bottom of the valley, marks the site of a pond, drained many years ago and now little more than a marsh. The remaining lake is known as the Great Pond and it soon comes into view. At this end it is also marshy and is a great spot for the birdwatcher. All types of waterfowl might be seen, from the tiny

Dabchick to the Mute Swan. There is always something swimming around, usually just too far away to be easily distinguished without binoculars.

On the right, you reach the impressive main gates of Stubbing Court, once the home of Lady Olive Baden-Powell, the World Chief Guide. Soon there is a glimpse of the frontage of the house through the park.

At the end of the Great Pond is Salem methodist chapel. This was built in 1849 for the people of Wingerworth. It was the nearest land that the methodists could find which was not owned by the catholic Hunloke family. One notable member of the chapel was John Norman, who was a fine violinist. He was wont to play for dances and this brought him into conflict with his fellow worshippers. Disgusted by their attempts to prevent his playing, he deserted the chapel and adopted the Church of England instead, becoming Churchwarden at the parish church of All Saints, Wingerworth.

Go left at the road junction and cross the dam. This is a public road and you should take care as it is very narrow and there is no footway. Fortunately most traffic is moving very slowly. At the far end of the dam go left at the junction. From this point, just before the boat house, is the most impressive view of Stubbing Court. The view from the house, down through the park and over the lake must be equally good and was obviously deliberately designed to be so.

Follow the road past the boat-house. When the road swings right, go straight on, through the stile by the gate and enter the field.

The right of way climbs gently to the right, to run along the upper edge of the field, just below the fence, with its convoluted trees and incipient rock outcrops. There is a grand view of Stubbing Pond from here. At the stile at the far end of the field, go into the wood which fringes the end of the pond. Keep close to the top of the bank, ignoring paths descending to the left. Birdwatchers using these lower paths have been known to stray into the morass at the head of the pond and have some difficulty in extracting themselves. Be warned!

Your path winds through the wood, which is carpeted with bluebells in Spring. Eventually, where the path comes close to the fence on the right, another track joins, rising steeply from the left. There are stiles ahead and right. Go right.

How Good is your Long Jump Technique?

Keeping the hedge on your left, head towards the gorse bushes. Before reaching them, at the gap in the hedge, there is an opportunity to test your long jump abilities as you seek to avoid a damp patch. On reaching the gorse bushes, seek out the stile in the left-hand corner of the field. Go over this stile and then immediately left, over another stile into a field used for "horsiculture". The next stile is just to the right of the trees, on the opposite side of the field.

The path then follows the edge of Green Wood, with a good view to the right over Chesterfield, before passing through another stile.

At this point, the wall enclosing the trees swings off left, while the path goes straight ahead, towards the electricity pole and the white gate in the next field. There are a further stile and another field of horses to be negotiated before the white gate is reached. Even when you get there the gate proves difficult to open. Negotiate it somehow and enter the fenced path alongside another area of woodland. This path ceases at a blue metal gate, which opens easily and reveals nothing more threatening than grazing sheep. Go right at this point, alongside the hedge, to a stile to the right of the monumental gateposts. The builder of both the gate and the stile obviously had delusions of grandeur. Perhaps he was connected with the fine house on the opposite side of the road. Go right at the road, and, just past the farm take the path through the stile on the left.

Despite indications to the contrary on the OS map, the path goes straight down the left-hand side of the field, to a new stile in the left-hand hedge. If you miss this final stile, there is another in the bottom left-hand corner. Go through the stile, turn right and continue down the field to the bottom. There, descend the steps to the little stone bridge over the brook.

A narrow path then leads away left, heading upstream to the corner of the fence which is on your right. At the corner, the path turns right, climbs the bank and goes through a stile with an ingenious hinged top bar. This stile leads into fields again.

On your right are the buildings of Broadgorse Farm, which have undergone extensive restoration and rebuilding. The path keeps to the right-hand side of the field to a gate by the propane tank. Just beyond the gate is a stile which takes you out onto the driveway for Broadgorse Farm. Here turn left.

Broadgorse Farm to Walton Lodge

Go along the driveway towards the main A632 road. As part of the farm reconstruction, the drive exit onto the main road has been moved about 50 metres to give better visibility. The old drive, which was,and still is, the public footpath, has been partially blocked at the end nearest the farm. The new drive is both easier to use and safer, but until there is an official diversion of the path you should use the right of way.

Cross the main road with care and go left along the frontage of Lodge Cottages. On the right, near the driveway to Walton Lodge, there is a stile in the wall. The field which you enter is very narrow at this point. Three bounds should see you across to the next stile. Two more bounds take you across the Walton Lodge drive to another stile. It must be quicker to walk round into the drive than negotiate two stiles, but the drive is not the right of way.

Leaving the drive behind, drop down to the trees with the hedge on your left, to reach a little waymarked gate. The path weaves its way through trees and scrub, crossing a couple of streams and muddy patches. Just after the second stream, the path bears away left on a waymarked route, through a tunnel in the holly bushes. What appears to be an obvious path, turns left and crosses the stream again before the holly tunnel, but a glance at the fences it negotiates will show that it is not made by human feet. Go up the holly tunnel, with the stream running in a steep sided gully on your left. Wind your way up through the woodland, in company with the brook, to a stile which brings you into open fields again.

Bear right here, alongside the barn of Walton Lodge Farm, heading up to the trees at the top of the hill. Here there is a double step stile, crossing a fence and a wall. It is cunningly designed to let you out but keep sheep in.

Once over the second stile, go right, alongside the wall and the trees. Continue alongside the wall, through another stile at the end of the line of trees and follow the sides of the field as it skirts the grounds of Walton Lodge. In the corner of this field is a blocked-up stile leading into the Walton Lodge grounds. Don't panic, but carry on, round the field to the left. You will soon reach a gateway and cross a stream into another field. Continue along the right-hand hedge of this field, with a good view over to Chesterfield on your right. There is a stile in the right-hand corner of the field.

Continue alongside the right-hand edge of the field, by the upper reaches of Old Spring Wood. Holymoorside and Old Brampton are now in view ahead. The exit from this field is not exactly in the right-hand corner, but slightly to the left, by a gate. Head across the next field towards the electricity pole and to the left of the clump of hawthorn. The indistinct path soon assumes the proportions of a track and heads down to a stile by a gate, just above the buildings of Rose Farm.

The stile gives out onto the farm road and a path is signed left. Ignore this and go right instead, through the gate across the farm road. Keep to the left of the main farm buildings and silos. At the next gateway, at the far end of the farm buildings, go straight on, again ignoring a stile on the left. Continue down the lane to the road.

Your way ahead lies over the stile with the fancy gold topped hand posts, to the left of Pine Lodge. (Just to the right of Pine Lodge is a small enclosed area with a fine array of daffodils at the appropriate season – to be admired, not picked)! The stile has been recently signed, so with the combination of gold posts and sign you shouldn't miss it! A second, more commonplace stile quickly follows, then the path keeps close to the hedge on the right, passing Pine Lodge.

A further stile, to the left of the electricity pole, takes the path round the north side of the farm buildings. Ignore the steep track going to the right which leads to a new and typically unattractive shed. Keep straight on, following the electricity wires through two more stiles into fields again. Holymoorside is now very close and the Bulls Head can be seen to the right.

Memories of A Mis-Spent Youth

Continue alongside the hedge. This steep field and the one below it, accessed by a rough gap in the hedge on your right, used to be the sledging fields for village youngsters. Some came to grief in the river at the bottom. Many more got no further than the gap or the holly hedge!

You are now on the last lap, but be wary, for there is a well-hidden ditch across the line of march. The ditch is crossed by a small stone slab bridge, then the path goes through a stile into a rough lane. The lane emerges onto the road exactly opposite the spot you left it some hours ago.

Go right, down the hill past the United Reform Chapel to the pub and bus stop or your car.

13: HUNDALL 28/10/95

The Route: Hundall – Woodsmithies Farm – Ramshaw Wood – Television Mast – Grasscroft Wood – Glasshouse Common – Stubbing Wood – Hundall

Distance: 2.6 miles (4.25km)

Start: Roadside parking on the Hundall – Unstone road, just below the Miners Arms. Grid reference: 385772

Map(s): OS 1:25000 Pathfinder Series No. 761, Chesterfield

How to get there:

By Public Transport: There is a Monday to Saturday bus service from Chesterfield.

By Car: Follow the B6057 to Unstone, then the signs to Apperknowle. Hundall is signed to the right at the next junction.

The Pub

The Miners Arms at Hundall has a commanding view over the valley. Worthington Beers are served on hand-pump and there are real fires in season. Wards, Stones and Smiths beers are also on offer, plus Murphy's Irish Stout. This is a friendly, welcoming pub with a room for walkers and families. The main bar boasts a collection of cricketing memorabilia and bank notes from around the world. The pub is also supposed to have a resident ghost. Food is served daily except Sundays. Opening hours are 11am – 4pm and 6.30pm – 11pm Monday to Friday, 11am – 5pm and 6.30pm – 11pm on Saturdays, 12noon – 3pm and 7pm – 10.30pm on Sundays.

The Walk

Leave the pub and descend the lane past Hundall Cottage. There is a fine view from here, right over the Drone valley to Owler Bar and the Peak District. Where the road goes right, by the chevron markings, there is a footpath sign to the left, pointing down a steep and narrow hollow-way. Go down this lane warily, for there's little chance to escape if a vehicle comes along. Fortunately they come but rarely and also slowly, so you should be all right. The lane widens out as you near Woodsmithies Farm and you pass to the left of the farm buildings, deviating neither to left or right. Carry straight on along what is by now a narrow track. On the right are the overgrown spoil heaps from Unstone Colliery. A multi waymarked post is reached and here you go straight on into the wood. At the fork of the track, in the wood, bear left and begin the climb out of the valley. On the right, in the trees, you can just discern the trackbed of the former railway which served the colliery.

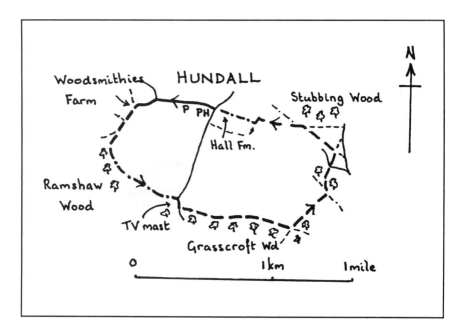

TV as a Waymarker

The path climbs quite steeply to a green gate, which is waymarked. Bear left here, still climbing, through the coppiced woodland with its carpet of bluebells. The path soon emerges from the wood into open fields. Continue upwards, with the woods on your right. Hundall and Apperknowle can be seen to the left. Part way up the field there is a waymarker which directs you left, across the field to the corner of the hedge. Then continue alongside the hedge, with the TV mast in view ahead. As you have now risen above the wood, there is a good view back across the valley. A number of the field boundaries shown on the map have been removed in this area, but the path is clear enough. Where the hedge does a right and left stagger, keep straight on, with the hedge to your left and the mast now to your right. Chesterfield can be seen away to the right.

Soon you reach a narrow lane and here you go right, towards the TV mast. Just before the mast, there is a track going off to the left, through a gate and stile. Follow this route up into fields again, then, keeping the hedge to your left, follow the path along the top edge of the field, with Grasscroft Wood below on the right. At the end of the field, there are paths going off into the wood, but your route keeps to the left-hand edge of the trees, passing through a stile. Keep straight on, with the wood to your right and the fence to your left, until you reach another stile by a white gate. Go through the stile, not the gate and so come out into fields again, though still with Grasscroft Wood on your right. Continue alongside the wood, through another stile, with an increasingly good view opening up ahead. At the next stile, there is a crossing of paths. Go left, not over the stile, and leave the wood behind.

A Tumbled Wilderness

Follow the indistinct path alongside the fence until you reach the corner of the field. Do not go through the stile on the right, but instead proceed through the gap in the fence ahead. This takes you into a tumbled wilderness, with a riot of trees and scrubby bushes of thorn and gorse. A broad track bears away to the left just inside the jungle, but your route lies to the right, almost straight ahead. It is a narrower track but distinct. It manoeuvres round hummocks and hollows, trees and bushes, tending gently downhill, until it reaches a stile.

The stile takes you out onto a narrow lane by a few houses. The right of way goes straight ahead, clipping the corner of the garden of one of the houses, though most walkers will tend to use the nearby lane and drive instead. Go through the stile to the right of the lamp post and thus enter fields again. An obvious path heads off across the field, making for the right hand corner of Stubbing Wood. In mid field there is an equally obvious crossing of paths and here you turn left, heading now for the left-hand corner of the wood. A stile in the corner of the field takes you out onto a narrow green lane. Go left here.

By Green Lane and Field Path to Hundall

Follow the lane, which soon does a sharp left and right wiggle. Ignore the path leading away to the right at this point and continue along the track. It is clearly used by horses and is churned up and muddy. Soon the television mast comes into view on the left, with Hundall also in view ahead. The lane now goes sharp left, apparently heading for the grass covered spoil heaps. After 50 metres, look out for a gap in the right-hand hedge. A jumble of stones and a post seems to suggest that there may have been a stile here at one time, but no longer. Go straight on, across the field, making for the red brick shed. The view is extensive, reaching over to the Peak District moors. A stile takes you through into another field, with the grass and tree covered spoil heap on the left. Still head for the shed. Another stile accesses a narrow path alongside the shed and the Miners Arms now comes into view. Go straight on to reach the road just above the pub.

14: KIRK LANGLEY

The Route: Kirk Langley Church – Flagshaw Lane – Buck Hazels –Smith's Plantation – Priestwood Farm – Meynell Langley – Bowbridge Fields Farm – Sandy Lane Farm – Langley Common – Kirk Langley Church

Distance: 5.1 miles (8.25km)

Start: Kirk Langley Church, Grid reference: 287388

Map(s): OS 1:25000 Pathfinder Series Nos. 811, Belper and 832, Derby and Etwall

How to get there:

By Public Transport: Daily bus service from Ashbourne, Derby and Manchester. Sunday service from Mansfield and Alfreton. In either case alight at the Meynell Arms.

By Car: The A52 from Derby or Ashbourne passes through Kirk Langley. To reach the car parking area by the church you should take the minor road opposite the Meynell Arms.

The Pub

The Blue Bell Inn, at Moor Lane, Langley Common is situated on the old Roman Road from Derby to Rocester. Not that the pub is quite that old, but it is a good honest local despite that. Bass and Marstons are the beers on offer and very good they are too. There's a small family area and a large beer garden. Please note that the play frame is for children and not for practising abseiling. Food is served at lunchtimes, Monday to Saturday and there are frequent weekend barbecues. Opening hours are 11.30am – 2.30pm and 5.30pm – 11pm Monday to Saturday, 12noon – 2.30pm and 7pm – 10.30pm on Sundays.

The Walk

The walk starts from Kirk Langley church. Either before or after the walk it is worth having a look in the church itself. It is dedicated to St. Michael and the present building dates back to the 14th century, though the tower is later. It contains interesting memorials to the two great landowning families of the area, the Meynells and the Poles. There is much ancient woodwork, especially the screen of the Meynell Choir. The village pound, where stray cattle were kept, is in Church Lane and here also is the old Mapple Well, once the village's water supply.

Walk down the road to the main A52, just opposite the Meynell Arms. This old coaching inn opens from 11am to 11pm Monday to Saturday and serves Bass beers. However, it is rather early in the walk to be thinking of imbibing. Cross the road with care and go left. Just past the village nameplate, by the ivy covered tree on the right, there is a stile. It is well hidden and has no sign post. It leads into a rough field, where you should bear left alongside the hedge to reach another stile in the far corner. Surprisingly this is waymarked. Now head towards the corrugated metal building on the left to reach a bridge in the corner of the field. This shows little sign of use, but it serves the purpose of getting you over the Flagshaw Brook dry-shod.

Langley Hall Farm

Once over the brook, continue up the left-hand side of the field, with the fence to your left. Just beyond the gnarled chestnut tree, there is a stile on the left. Negotiate this and then bear right, keeping to the right of the buildings of Langley Hall Farm. Head for the stile in the hedge to the right of the buildings. At the time of the author's visit, this stile was partially obstructed with barbed wire. Having extricated yourself from this predicament you will arrive on Flagshaw Lane.

Go straight across the lane to a stile, which takes you back into fields again. Continue straight ahead to reach a stile in the fence cum hedge, between the mast and the tree. The stile is also marked by the tallest post in the fence. Despite being shown on the OS map, some of these hedges and fences look surprisingly new. Clamber over the stile, through the hedge and over another stile to reach the next field. Quite a performance! Bear right down the next field, heading for the far right-hand corner. There is a culvert here, over a small stream and then you reach a gate. Go through the gate into the next field, heading straight on,

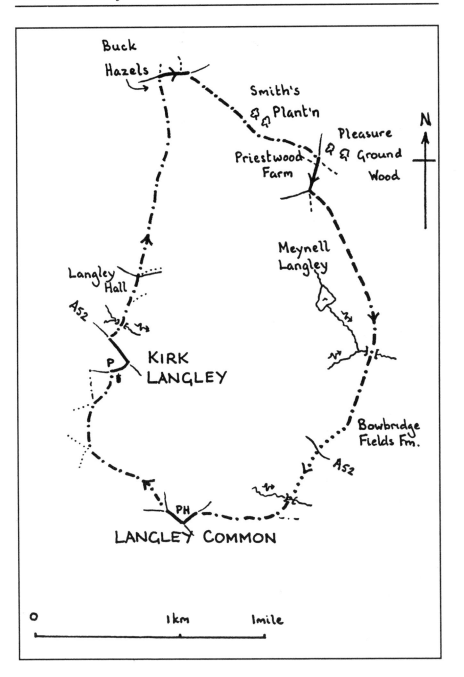

Buck Hazels

Smith's Plant'n

Pleasure Ground Wood

Priestwood Farm

N

Meynell Langley

Langley Hall

A52

P

KIRK LANGLEY

Bowbridge Fields Fm.

A52

PH

LANGLEY COMMON

0   1km   1mile

towards the third electricity pole from the left, the one in the trees. The field boundaries shown on the OS map have gone, but there is the semblance of a walked path. The exit stile is to the left of the ash tree at the far end of the field. Once over this stile, bear diagonally left across the next field heading to the right of the buildings of Buck Hazels Farm. There is a stile beside the gate in the new fence before you reach the farm. Keep straight on, to the right of the house and to the left of the little brick hut. Ignore the farm track and gate and locate a stile in the hedge, just near the little hut. Go over this stile into the lane and turn right.

Proceed along the lane for about 200 metres, then where it bends to the left, heading towards Kedleston, go right, into the fields again, through a wide gap in the hedge by the ash tree. There is quite an extensive view from this point over Kedleston Park, although Kedleston Hall cannot be seen as it is hidden by trees. Quarndon Water Tower is a prominent landmark.

Discrepancies on The Map

The map shows the path running parallel to the right-hand hedge of the field, but about 50 metres in from the edge. In practice the path seems to stick more closely to the hedge, passing to the right of the remnants of the pond instead of to the left as shown on the map. Keep alongside the hedge at the top of the field, leaving Smith's Plantation away to your left. There is a gap in the hedge ahead, between the ash tree and the chestnut. This is the route out of the field. There is no stile. Ahead you can now see Priestwood Farm. The path heads towards the left of the buildings, to a stile marked by a tall post. Skirt the farm to reach another stile by the gate and then head across the field to a further stile, by the holly tree and close to the cattle trough. The map actually shows the right of way bearing right at this point to utilise the farm drive, but that is clearly not what happens in practice.

At the stile by the holly, you reach the Kedleston – Kirk Langley road and turn right. Ignore the signpost on the left opposite the drive to Priestwood Farm and continue on the lane, dipping down to cross the stream. There is a fine view into Derby from here. You can clearly see the Cathedral and the newly-created University.

A well-defended Path

Climb up from the stream, still on the road. Where the lane bends sharply to the right, by the lodge, go left, not down the drive to Meynell Langley House, but onto the track in the adjoining field. The pill box is presumably a wartime remnant, not an attempt to stop would-be walkers using the path. The author was not challenged when testing out this route! Continue down the track, with the boundary hedge of Meynell Langley House on the right. Pass through two gateways and skirt another pillbox. On the right now is the parkland belonging to Meynell Langley House. There is a stile in the boundary fence on the right, but this is not a right of way, so ignore it, continuing alongside the hedge and fence. In this manner you will soon reach a stile in the hedge ahead. Negotiate this and continue alongside the Park boundary, noting the ornamental pond on your right. Near the end of this field, the Park boundary hedge and fence begins to bend to the right. Your route lies straight ahead, to a stile in line with the water tower, seen on the horizon.

In the next field there are remains of ridge and furrow farming. The Park boundary swings away to the right and the footpath also bears right, towards the big tree in the far hedge. The stile lies to the left of the tree. Now go straight ahead down this next field, to reach a bridge just to the right of the willow tree. Cross the stream and head up the field towards the right-hand end of the buildings of Bowbridge Fields Farm. There is a good view back from here, to Meynell Langley House, the frontage of which can be clearly seen from this vantage point. As the name suggests, the owners of the Meynell Langley estate are the Meynells, who have been in possession since the time of Henry I.

The path passes through a gateway to the left of a tree and then continues upwards, with the fence on the left, until you are almost at the farm. At the gate by the trough, go right, through another gate towards the telegraph pole, leaving the farm away to your left. The field ahead is pathless, but has sure signs of ridge and furrow farming, so much so that a traverse of this area is more akin to a sea crossing than walking. Go diagonally right across this field, heading to the far right-hand corner. After some disconcerting moments you will find a stile, well hidden in the hawthorn hedge. This deposits you neatly onto the main A52 road.

A Worrying Approach to a Stream

Turn right, along the road and then almost at once (before you reach the farm), go left, through the gate into the field. There is a fine parish boundary marker in the verge at this point. Go down the field, keeping the hedge to your right, and so reach a gate in the bottom right-hand corner. There is no stile, nor is there much sign of previous pedestrian use. Bear diagonally right across the next field, though there is no sign of any exit at the bottom. Doubts begin to mount as you approach the stream, but then you will spot a cunningly hidden footbridge, right in the corner. Incredibly, it turns out to be waymarked!

On the Roman Road

Cross the footbridge and ascend the slope on the far side of the stream, bearing right as you go, to reach a stile in the right-hand hedge, where the boundary does a left and right kink. At this point you are on the alignment of the Roman Road of Long Lane. This ran from the fort at Derby to the fort at Rocester on the Dove. For much of its length it is still in use as a motor road. Other sections, like this one, are footpaths.

The path follows the Roman line straight across the next rough little field. Go over the stile in the fence and continue straight ahead again, heading to the left of the brick built house and the new planting. The pub is now in view ahead. The path dips to cross a muddy trickle and there is a stile to the left of the ash tree. Follow the right-hand fence up by the drive to reach another stile by the holly tree. Thus you enter a narrow lane, still on the Roman alignment. Follow the lane until you reach the Blue Bell Inn.

Kirk Langley in View

On leaving the pub, turn right and go along the road to its junction with Long Lane. There is no footway so proceed with care. At the junction, there is a footpath sign in the angle between Moor Lane and Long Lane, just by the 7.5 tonne weight limit sign. Go over the stile at this point and bear diagonally right across the field. The spire of Kirk Langley church is in view ahead and to the right. The path makes for a gateway in the far right-hand corner of the field. Here you join a short length of green lane, which drops sharply down to cross a culverted stream. Beyond the stream the path rises again, with the hedge on your right. Go straight up the field, keeping about 50 metres from the right-hand hedge, which soon does a series of kinks to come and join you. There is some rough land on the left, which looks like old mineral workings of some description, but the map throws no light on this, but suggests that there should be a pond here.

Keep alongside the right-hand hedge and so reach a waymarked stile by a gate. There is a crossing of paths at this point but none are particularly obvious on the ground. Go right and into another field, now heading for the church tower. Another stile by a gate takes you into the long field, shown on the map as leading right down to the church. This does not prove to be the case in practice, for there is a new fence and tree planting part way down. Negotiate the stile provided, then head towards the right-hand corner of the field. Here you will find a gate, just by the churchyard. The gate leads into a narrow lane and thence to the road and your car.

The Blue Bell Inn

15: LITTLE EATON

The Route: Bell and Harp – Eatonpark Wood – Daypark – Portway –Coxbench Station Crossing – Coxbench – Horsley Grange – Horsley – Golden Valley – Hilltop Farm – Smalley Mill Road – Cloves Hill – Marks Hill –Brackley Gate – Horsley Carr – Toad Lane – Bell and Harp

Distance: 6.4 miles (10.25km)

Start: The start is the Bell and Harp pub. The bus stops outside, or limited parking is available in a small layby opposite The Chase. Grid reference: 367427

Map(s): OS 1:25000 Pathfinder Series No. 811. Belper

How to get there:

By Public Transport: daily bus services from Derby, Chesterfield and Ripley.

By Car: from the south, A38/A61 junction signed Little Eaton. Pass through Little Eaton following the signs to Coxbench and Holbrook.

The Pub

The Bell and Harp at Little Eaton is a fine old village pub serving the full range of Marstons Beers, including Pedigree and Best Bitter on hand pump. There is a small beer garden overlooking the old main road. There are two bars, the larger being the public bar which has several different levels, a real fire and a tiled floor, so no need to worry about clean boots. Families are welcome at lunchtimes, especially at weekends. Unusually, the pub does not do food, but it has a roaring trade despite that. For the past 25 years the pub has been the headquarters of the local tug of war team. There are pictures and trophies around the walls commemorating previous triumphs. An excellent local.

The Walk

This walk can be divided into two short strolls, or taken as one long hike. Either way, the starting point and the pub are the same. From the Bell and Harp, go right for a short distance along the Alfreton Road until you reach the junction with Whittaker Lane. This is signed as a bridleway, so turn right here and head up the lane. The lane climbs steadily and after the last house, by the corrugated iron garage and the stables, it ceases to be tarred and becomes a narrow muddy track.

An Old Bridleway

The bridleway proceeds more steeply uphill, keeping to the edge of the trees of Eaton Park Wood. The hill gradually eases and the path then bears right to go through the wood. There is no risk of going wrong here as the path is clearly defined and, for the most part is fenced or walled on either side. The track emerges from the wood and there is a stile to the left and a blue waymarker pointing straight on. Ignore both of these and instead take the narrow path to the right, negotiating the strategically placed fallen tree to find a stile in the wall.

Go through the stile into the field and bear left, heading for the right-hand end of the clump of trees, seen on the horizon. There is a good view to the right from here, over towards Horsley and Kilburn. Close by there is also a substantial stone building which seems curiously out of place but well maintained, though with no obvious agricultural or domestic function. The field is one of those with a slight rise in the middle of it, just enough to hide the far boundary from view. Eventually, you will spot two posts and these mark the site of the exit stile and gate.

Derwent Aqueduct 1

Go through the stile and, keeping the fence to your right, head towards the right-hand end of the clump of trees to reach another stile. The path now skirts the eastern end of Daypark Wood, which the OS map shows as being a former quarry, though it's not obvious on the ground. Best to stick to the path though and not investigate too closely. At the end of the wood the path reaches a stile, well protected by a holly bush. In the next field, head towards the stone post and big oak tree. As you near the stone post you will see that it holds up a green metal gate and that there is a prominent terrace running from this gate across the field in the direction of the stone building you saw earlier. If you have done much

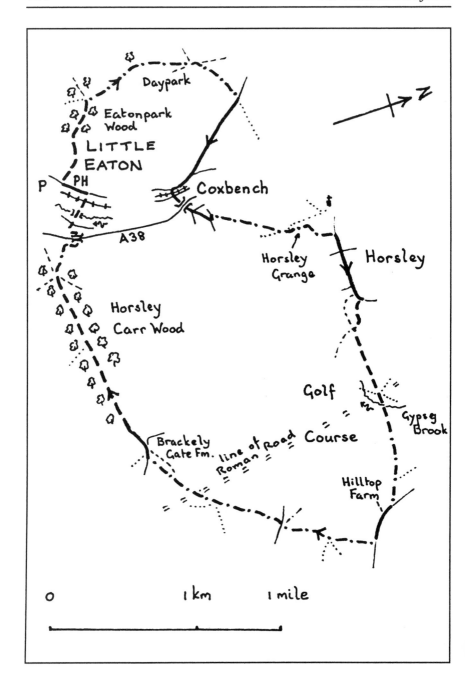

walking in the Peak District, the sight of the green gate should jog your memory, for here you are on the alignment of the great Derwent Aqueduct. The stone building is one of the many valve houses and the gate gives access to water company employees inspecting and maintaining the pipes. Do not go through the gate, but skirt round to the right, by the oak, through a gap in the hedge and into another field. Bear right across this field, which shows obvious remains of ridge and furrow farming, towards a stile by a gate in the far right-hand corner, by the buildings.

The Saxon Portway and St. Anthony's Well

Once through the gate you enter a narrow lane with houses on the left-hand side. In a very short distance there are two gates on the right. Alongside the second is a very overgrown stile, but this is of little concern as the gate is usually open anyhow. Go into the field and bear left, heading diagonally across the meadow towards a clump of trees. When the fence and hedge at the bottom of the field are reached, you will need to cast along it to the left to find the stile. This takes you into a very small field, with a hedge on the left. At the end of this field is another stile to the left of the breeze block building. The path then runs between a garden on the left and a house on the right to reach the road.

The road is known as the Portway, a name of some considerable historic significance, for this route has been in use, with that name since at least Saxon times. It can be traced from the county boundary near Ilkeston, through Belper and Wirksworth to Bakewell and Castleton. It would make a grand medium distance walk in its own right, but today your route only touches a small part of it. Go right along the road to the junction and there bear right, passing Coxbench Hall. Just beyond the hall there is another road junction. It will not take a genius with a map to realise that a continuation down the main road will soon bring you back to the Bell and Harp. This is the way to go if you need to cut the walk short, but the full route turns left at the junction, going down the lane to Coxbench level crossing and the former railway station. Both the station buildings and the crossing are remarkable survivals of the good old days of railways – very nostalgic.

Leaving the crossing behind, negotiate the old A61 road, which is a lot less busy than it used to be, but every bit as fast as it ever was, so take care. On the other side of the old road go under the new A38 using the bridge kindly provided by the Department of Transport. Immediately on the far side of the bridge, there is a curious little stone structure. A

plaque proclaims that this is (or was) St. Anthony's Well and that it
dates back to 1611. It has, of course, been moved, presumably as a result
of the new road. Bear left past the well, up the lane.

After about 200 metres, the lane begins to level out and you near the last
houses. Another, even narrower lane trails in from the left. Go sharp left
here and then, just beyond Rock Cottage, go right, up a flight of steps
which seem to be leading into the back garden of the cottage. Instead the
steps lead to a waymarked stile into a field. Bear right across the field
towards the barn and gate. The next field is the abode of horses, some of
the decidedly frisky variety, but otherwise harmless enough. You are
also likely to be seen on your way by a number of dogs, but again they
are playful rather than vicious. Head across the field to a kissing gate
part way up the opposite hedge and so leave the horses and dogs
behind.

Head for Horsley Church Spire

In the next field the path keeps to the same general alignment, heading
to the left of the pylon to a stile in the top hedge. At this point Horsley
Church comes into view ahead and is a useful marker. The church was
built in the 14th century but has been much "restored". The path runs
diagonally across the field to a couple of posts. These turn out to be old
gate posts, now minus gate, but here the path turns left to pass through
another gateway. Continue ahead, keeping the hedge to your right. Two
paths cross this field. The more obvious heads for the church, but your
route keeps alongside the right-hand hedge, avoiding the old farm
machinery and the fallen tree. As you draw level with Horsley Grange
on your right, there are a gateway and a stile. Ignore these, as they only
lead into the farmyard, and continue beside the hedge to reach another
stile. Negotiate this and then head across the little field to the left of the
buildings. Just by the buildings, when there seems to be no way out, the
path turns abruptly left and passes down a narrow ginnel, with a hedge
on one side and a fence on the other. In this manner you reach the main
road in Horsley village. Go right here.

Horsley

Horsley gives its name to the Horsley Cup, which is nothing to do with
horses at all, but is an annual church bell-ringing competition. Rivalry
between the different ringing teams can be very fierce and points are
awarded both for technical accuracy and for the difficulty of the ringing
method chosen. The church itself is a Saxon foundation dedicated to St.

Clement and St. James, but the present building is mainly 13th and 14th century. There was a royal castle at Horsley from the reign of King John to that of Queen Mary Tudor. It was a surprising distance from the village and although the site is shown on the OS map, there is nothing much to see.

The road leads past the Blanche Well, on French Lane. This well was one of three, donated by Rev. Sitwell, then vicar of Horsley in 1864. The wells were named after his three daughters, Blanche, Sophie and Rosamund. Here also is a stone pillar box, in use from 1869 – 87. Continue along the main street to the triangular junction by the Coach and Horses, a Marstons house. Continue the main road, past the pub until you reach a gap in the modern houses on the right-hand side of the road. There is a public footpath sign here, directing you down the gap and this is your route. At the bottom of the gardens, there is a stile by a gate and the path enters fields again.

Once in the field, bear left to reach a stile half way down the hedge. Beyond this stile the path forks. Go straight on towards the overgrown spoil heap. (The route to the right may seem to be shorter on the map and this is so, but for most of the way it passes across a golf course, so it is not recommended). Pass to the right of the spoil heap to a derelict stile and then keep alongside the hedge. The houses of Horsley Woodhouse soon appear on the skyline to the left, while to the right is the golf course. Keep alongside the hedge through a series of fields, all with stiles in place, until you reach a pond on the right. The path skirts the pond to a plank footbridge and a stile.

Potential Confusion

The next field is rather confusing. There is a stile on the right, but you should ignore this. Ahead, the hedge is breached by two gaps, both with attendant holly trees. Go for the smaller, left-hand gap, which also has the smaller of the two hollies. Again, the next field seems to present a choice. To the right there is a broad gap in the hedge. This should be disregarded. To the left a footbridge can be seen in the field corner by the line of willows and this is your route. Cross the Gypsy Brook by the footbridge. Now go up the field, with the hedge on your left, to reach a gap in the top corner, by the tree stump. Go left here and follow the hedge on your right until you reach a stile. Negotiate the stile and go left, beside the hedge to the footbridge in the corner of the field. Bear right in the next field, heading diagonally across towards the buildings of Hilltop Farm. With luck you will locate a stile and a plank footbridge

about half way up the opposite hedge/fence. Continue to head for
Hilltop Farm, bearing right across the field. There is a stile in the top
right-hand corner. Follow the hedge on your right to a stile which takes
you out onto the road and here go right.

Go up the road, passing Hilltop Farm on your right. Ignore the footpath
sign on the left and continue almost to the Sitwell Arms. The Sitwell
Arms is a Bass House, which provides food from 12noon – 2pm,
Tuesdays to Saturdays. Just before the pub there is a footpath sign on
the opposite side of the road and this is your route. Go into the field and
follow the left-hand hedge. There is a series of well built stiles to be
climbed in the next few fields. The OS map shows this a one large field.
Looking across the valley you can discern the line of the Roman Road,
Ryknield Street, which shows as a diagonal line running uphill from
right to left in a couple of fields. You will meet this route later in the
walk. Keep the hedge on your left until you nearly reach the bottom of
the third field. There is a gap in the hedge ahead and a stile in the hedge
on the left, but your route lies to the right, cutting off the corner of the
field to a footbridge over a stream which serves as the field boundary.
Here go left, alongside a hedge again, noting the overgrown remains of
buildings and spoil heaps in the field on the left. At the next stile, in a
new fence, not on the map, bear right. You will soon spot the footbridge,
to the right of the gate and to the left of the old caravan.

The Ryknield Street

Just beyond the footbridge the path goes up to the stile by the gate and
so reaches Smalley Mill Road. Cross the road and negotiate the stile
signed to Cloves Hill. Once over the stile, keep by the hedge and tree
belt on the right to reach another stile in the far corner of the field.
Beyond this stile the land rises quite steeply and the far boundary of the
field cannot be seen, neither is there any obvious sign of a path. This is
all the more disconcerting as the map shows two paths through this
field. Continue straight ahead up the bank towards the two small
hawthorns and soon the field boundary comes into view, and the stile in
the far corner. It is worth stopping at the top of the hill, which is not
Cloves Hill at all but Marks Hill, to admire the view and survey the
ground. The view is surprisingly extensive. Crich Stand and the radio
masts on Alport Hill can be seen to the north west. Beside the hedge a
broad hollow runs down the field in a northerly direction. This is the
line of the Ryknield Street, mentioned earlier. Now go through the stile.
The route of the Roman Road is not obvious in this field. Your route
keeps alongside the right-hand wall to another stile in the corner. There

is a gateway on the right here, and an obvious track leading to the farm, but the stile takes you onto a field path, not through the farm yard.

Down the Brackley Gate

With Brackley Gate Farm on your right, head across the field, veering to the left, to reach a stile by the gate which exits onto the road. Here go right. At the road junction, the main road goes right, but your way lies straight ahead, down the lane marked with the No Through Road sign. This is the Brackley Gate, an ancient routeway. Once past the houses, the tarmac ceases and the lane becomes a fine hollow-way. It descends steeply through a delightful mixed woodland, quite rough and muddy underfoot. At the bottom of the first steep section there is evidence that the route is attempted by motor vehicles, but unless you are very unfortunate you'll not see any. The woodland on the right is Horsley Carr. The "carr" element of the name normally denotes a marshy area, but this wood is on a very steep slope so the name may be "displaced".

The track, walled on either side, runs steadily down towards the valley of the Bottle Brook. After the footpath sign on the left, which you ignore, you will begin to hear the rumble of traffic on the still hidden A38.

Derwent Aqueduct 2

A green metal gate on the right denotes the route of the great Derwent Aqueduct and soon afterwards, the trees on the right cease and there is a view over the valley. Passing the gateway on the left, leading into the Scout camp site at Drum Hill, the track begins to descend more steeply, soon becoming a tarred lane again. Another track trails in from the right and just beyond this there is an area of rough land to the right. Leave the lane at this point, bearing right and descending to cross another track before reaching a kissing gate. Tradition suggests that you should kiss the person who comes through behind you so choose you walking companions with care!

Derwent Aqueduct 3 and back to
The Bell and Harp

Descend through the field with the wall on your right towards the green inspection covers, which mark the course of the Derwent Aqueduct. At the bottom of the field, by the A38, go through a stile on the right and continue at the bottom of the road embankment to a green gate. The path goes left here, passing underneath the A38. On the far side of the bridge is one of the standard stone-built valve houses of the Derwent Aqueduct. The path goes left, again running along the bottom of the road embankment until a stile is reached on the right. Here the path leaves the new road behind and passes an old stone building on the left before reaching the former A61, now downgraded but still a fast road. Cross with care and go straight on to a footbridge over the stream. Imperceptibly you have also crossed the alignment of the Little Eaton Tramway, which ran from pits and iron works in the Ripley area to join the Derby Canal. It operated from 1793 to 1908. Cross the stream and the railway line to reach a track known as Toad Lane. This soon disgorges onto the old Alfreton road, the original main road! Here go left and follow the road back to the Bell and Harp.

16: LONG LANE

The Route: Long Lane School – Osleston Hall – Butt House – Sharrow Hall Farm – Windlehill Farm – The Elms – Osleston Medieval Village – Clover Fields – Long Lane School

Distance: 4.2 miles (6.75km)

Start: Outside Long Lane School, Grid reference: 252381

Map(s): OS 1:25000 Pathfinder Series No. 832, Derby and Etwall

How to get there:

By Public Transport: An extremely sparse bus service on Tuesdays Wednesdays and Fridays only, from Osmaston to Derby.

By Car: A515 from Ashbourne to Cubley, then follow the signs to Alkmonton. Long Lane is beyond Alkmonton. From Derby, follow the A52 almost to Kirk Langley, then go left to Langley Common and follow the "Long Lane".

The Pub

The Three Horseshoes at Long Lane is a fine white painted pub, selling Marstons and guest beers. It also serves food except Tuesdays and Sundays and has a beer garden, with a children's corner. A new family room is intended. Opening hours are 11.30am – 3.00pm and 6.00pm – 11.00pm Monday to Saturday, with the usual Sunday hours. The pub is unusual in that it is owned by a consortium of villagers who rescued it from proposed closure about three years ago. A real local.

The Walk

This was the thirteenth walk the author reconnoitred for this book and the route which appears here bears little resemblance to that originally intended. There were innumerable obstructions, ranging from a single strand of barbed wire, through a well grown hawthorn hedge, to a large brick built garage! Hopefully, the walk now described is both passable and enjoyable.

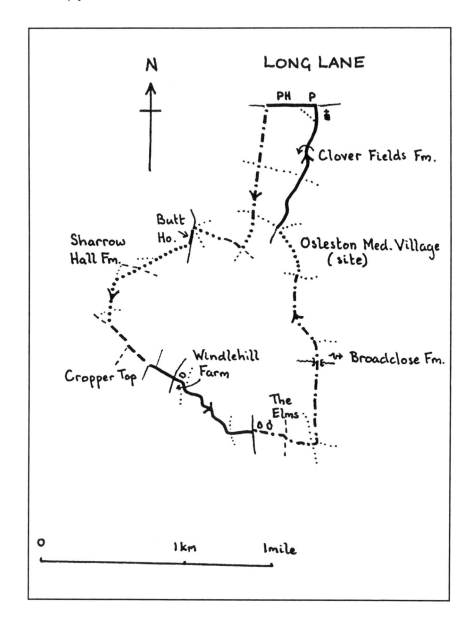

An "Interesting" Plank Bridge

From the pub go right, along Long Lane, which is a fine example of a Roman Road still in everyday use. The road dips to cross a small bridge and then, just past the stream there is a footpath sign on the left and a stile in the hedge. Leave the road at this point and go into the fields. Keep the hedge on your left and ignore the inviting gateway, noting instead the ample evidence of ridge and furrow farming in the field. At the end of the field there is another inviting gateway, facing you in the corner, but this is not the route you want. Instead, keep to the right of the gate (the hedge does a kink at this point) and keep on to the true end of the field, where you will find a stile. Straight on in this next field, again with the hedge to the left to reach another stile in the corner. The path goes into the next field and then immediately turns right, to pass through another stile. This is not as shown on the map. Go left at this point and resume your route with the hedge on your left. The hedge soon turns sharp left and the map suggests a field boundary at this point, but this has long gone. Carry straight on across the field, heading for a stile to the right of the big ash tree. Before reaching the stile there is a plank bridge over a small stream. The planks have seen better days and look decidedly rotten. Don't say you weren't warned.

Once over bridge and stile go straight up the middle of the field, which again has evidence of ridge and furrow, to reach a gate. Similarly in the next field, go straight up the middle, to another gate. The map shows that there is a crossing of paths in the midst of this field, but you'll need extremely good vision to spot any sign of it. The author was more concerned to avoid the attentions of the herd of cows, which persisted in following him across the field. Go through the next gate into another field. Osleston Hall Farm is on your left. Pass the remains of a pond on your left and continue across the field to a stile in the opposite hedge. This drops you into a narrow sunken lane. An obvious path goes straight on, but your route lies to the right along a very overgrown track. This soon reaches a fence, in which there is no stile, but which is readily climbed and after that the track finishes and you are in fields again. The map implies a route across the field. From what little evidence there is on the ground, it seems that walkers follow the right-hand hedge for about 50 paces, then go left, heading towards a clump of bushes and to the right of the house. The clump turns out to be the remains of a hedge and this you keep to your left, to reach a gate onto the road, by a derelict barn. There is a footpath sign at this point, so at least you have emerged in the right place, though the means of getting there might be dubious.

A Peculiar Trig Point

Go left at the road and pass Butt House on the right. The map suggests that the path you were following from Osleston Hall emerges onto the road at this point. It is gratifying to note that there is no sign of it at all. However, just past the house, on the right there is an overgrown stile by a gate. It is a matter for debate whether to risk the stile or to try and open the gate. The gate won in the author's case. The inconspicuous path heads diagonally across the field to a metal gate just to the left of an ash tree and the pond. Keep straight on, but towards the left-hand side of the field. The view to the right is quite extensive, but of more pressing urgency is how to get out of this field. The left-hand hedge has a curious kink in it and at this point there is a gap, as if there has been a gateway at some time. There is now a single strand barbed wire fence, which has no stile in it, but which can be easily negotiated. These exertions bring you into a much bigger field, with a pond to the left and a concrete building to the right. According to the map, the building is a trig point!

The buildings of Sharrow Hall Farm can now be seen ahead. The path is still indecipherable on the ground, but heads to the left of the buildings, to a gap in the far hedge. Three-quarters of the way across the field, you cross the drive leading to the farm, but don't deviate from your course. A pond now comes into view. Keep to the right of this and head for the gap in the far corner of the field. This proves to be a very muddy exit in a short narrow lane, which goes left into the next field. There is again no obvious path in this field, but the left-hand hedge kinks to the right and then to the left. If you follow this hedge, you will find a stile, well defended by nettles, but marked by an electricity pole and lying just to the left of the house.

Lots of Ponds and Few Paths

Go straight on to reach the next stile, with the hedge to your right and continue across the next field to a further stile. In this field comes the parting of ways between the walk as originally proposed and the walk which appears in this book. Head straight across the field to reach a farm track and here turn left. Follow the track, which soon becomes a narrow tarred lane until you reach the cross roads beyond Cropper Top Farm. At the cross roads go straight ahead past Hillcrest to reach another cross roads by Windlehill Farm. Again you go straight on here passing the lovely little pond on the left. There are a surprising number of ponds on this walk and the map shows a myriad of little blue dots in this area. Continue down the lane, which sees very little traffic, passing Tithe Barn

Cottage, and wriggling round the series of 'S' bends. Soon you reach a T-junction and here go left for a very short distance, less than 50 metres, before diverging to the right through a gate. There is no footpath sign of course, but then be thankful there's a gate!

In the field, keep to the right of the pond and thus reach a "stile" in the hedge. The stile is cunningly disguised as a piece of fence. In the next field, still keep to the right of the pond and the house, crossing the drive to The Elms to arrive at a gate in the opposite hedge. Incredibly, across the next field a stile can be seen and you head for this. There is a nasty surprise here in the form of a ditch which has to be jumped, but this manoeuvre lands you in a narrow field, which according to the map has several footpaths in it. Not that you would notice! Bear left and cross the field to reach a gate in the opposite hedge. Once through the gate go left alongside the hedge. A water tower is a prominent landmark ahead.

This is a long field, which dips gently down to a stream. Keep the hedge to your left and just before the stream there is a stile. Stiles have been something of a luxury on this walk and this one is even waymarked. However, it has its guardian nettle population well established. Beyond the stile lies the stream, which is bridgeless, but fortunately narrow. Continue up, away from the stream, but still with the hedge to your left. Almost at the top of the field, near the big ash tree, there is a tempting gate on the left. Ignore it and carry on. The hedge does a right and left kink at this point and thus reaches another gate, which is waymarked!

A Deserted Village

Go diagonally left across the next field to a stile to the left of an ash tree. An obvious route alongside the fence on the left turns out to be wrong, for there is an easily-missed, though waymarked stile in the left-hand fence. Once over this, go right, alongside the fence to reach another stile to the left of the first ash. Now go straight ahead to a stile in the middle of the far hedge, by the three trees. Beyond this stile, keep the hedge on your left and thus find another stile which takes you into the site of the lost village of Osleston. The tumbled ground is all that remains of this medieval village and it is hard to imagine that a thriving little settlement once stood on this spot. Keep straight on, with the hedge on your right, until you reach what has once been an old hedge across your path. Here bear left, diagonally across the village site to reach a stile, invisible from the other side of the field, but marked by two big trees. This returns you to the road and here you turn right. (If you wish to avoid further road walking, the signed path opposite returns you to your outward route).

Continue along the road, noting only the curious roof patterning of Long Lane church and the almost inevitable fact that the footpath, marked on the map as cutting left across the field to the pub, doesn't exist.

You emerge from the lane by the school. The pub lies just down the road to the left.

The Three Horseshoes

17: OSMASTON 22|10|95

The Route: Osmaston Village Hall – Osmaston Pond – Home Farm –Shirley Park Wood – Greaves Wood – Wyaston Grove – Wyaston Brook – Copse Hill – Osmaston village

Distance: 4 miles (6.5km)

Start: Osmaston Village Hall Car park, Grid reference: 199439

Map(s): OS 1:25000 Pathfinder Series Nos. 810, Ashbourne and Churnet Valley and 811, Belper

How to get there:

By Public Transport: There is a Thursday only service from Ashbourne to the village, but there is a daily service to Osmaston Lane End from Ashbourne, Derby and Manchester.

By Car: A52 from Derby or Ashbourne to Osmaston Lane End, then follow signs to the village.

The Pub

The Shoulder of Mutton at Osmaston is an idyllic pub in an equally idyllic village setting. It is open Monday to Saturday, 11.30am – 2.30pm and 7.00pm – 11.00pm, except Thursdays when it is closed at lunchtime. On Sundays, opening hours are 12.00noon – 3.00pm and 7.00pm – 10.30pm. Kirkby Strong Ales and Wards Sheffield beers are on offer and food is available at lunchtimes. Families and walkers are made very welcome and there is a garden area. The landlord points out that the pub has no juke box, to which one can only say "Thank Goodness".

The Walk

The walk begins in the delightful village of Osmaston, with its thatched houses and Village Hall, its Village Green and pond. Domesday Book records this village as "Osmundestune". Until 1843 the church was built of wickerwork, but between 1843-5 the new church of St. Martin's was built, to the design of the local architect, Stevens. Many thatched cottages remain in this charming village, but they are relatively modern, being part of a major rebuilding project undertaken by the Wright family who held the estate in the mid 19th century. Osmaston Manor was built at the same time, but was demolished in 1964 when the then owners, the Walker-Okeovers, moved to Okeover Hall near Mappleton.

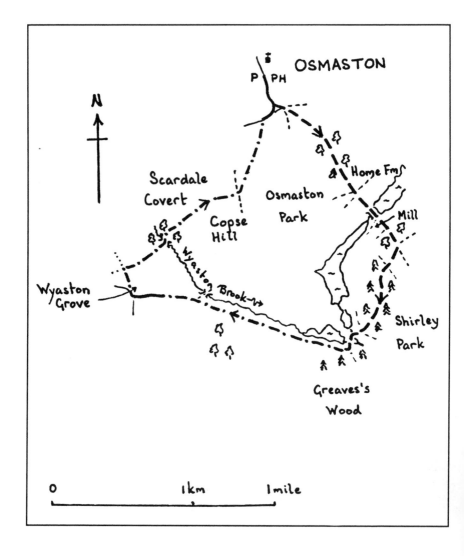

Walk down the road from the car park to the pond. There is a seat here made of horseshoes welded together. Ignore this, because it is far too early in the expedition to be thinking of sitting down and in any case the seat looks decidedly uncomfortable. Go left at the pond and where the road leads off left and right, go straight ahead on the route signed "Bridlepath to Shirley". The route to the right leads into Osmaston Park, while that to the left goes down Madge Lane to Shirley Bridge. Neither of these is any use to you.

Osmaston Village

Along the Shirley Bridlepath

There is no difficulty in following the Shirley Bridlepath. It is wide and well defined, being used by estate vehicles as well as walkers and horse riders. The track passes through a clump of trees, then meets another track, trailing in from the left. Keep straight on, through another tree clump to emerge just above Home Farm. The bell tower of the farm buildings is seen to the left. The track now begins to·descend quite sharply towards the string of lakes in the bottom of the valley. These lakes are all artificial, being part of the landscaped park of the former

Osmaston Hall. Keep straight on, over the 'crossroads' and then across the dam wall.

A Good Use of Ornamental Ponds

In best estate tradition, the water features in the park were not purely ornamental. They supplied fish and waterfowl for the table, while the power stored in the dammed water was used to operate the sawmills. As you reach the far side of the dam, the mill is on your right, complete with water wheel. Alas, it now seems to be derelict.

The way up from the dam is again signed to Shirley. The track ascends quite steeply, through the trees until it eventually levels out. You will notice various tracks and paths leading off left and right, but ignore these. Most of them have notices of some description warning you that the land is private. At the top of the hill, the track emerges from the woods at the point where five routes converge. The Shirley bridleway goes straight on, but your route is the next one to the right, along a muddy forest ride. This soon begins to descend again, heading generally south west, though it is hard to get ones bearings in the woods. Again there are various paths and tracks going off, but these are private and usually there are notices to say so. The woods are alive with game birds, including a number of white pheasants.

A Slippery Bridge

Where the track begins to level out there is a crossing of routes. Your way still lies straight ahead, towards the noise of a waterfall. Suddenly, the path comes out of the trees to cross the outfall stream from one of the lakes. There are a ford and a bridge by the waterfall. The lake lies to the right, but it can scarcely be seen. The ford is too deep for comfort, while the bridge is slippery. Be warned, you could easily become very wet here. Just over the bridge, the track forks. Go left along the waymarked route and thus come to a second ford and bridge, with a waterfall to the right. There is a stile just a short way ahead, by a gate. This takes you out of the parkland and back into open fields again.

Birdwatchers Paradise

In the field the route you need bears right, keeping close company with the edge of the lake. There is some evidence of an engineered terrace higher up the field, parallel to the more obvious path in the bottom, but the right of way is clearly shown on the OS map to be the lower path. This is a lovely stretch, with a wealth of birdlife on the lake.

Soon you reach the head of the lake. There is an area of marsh here, through which the feeder stream runs. Again this is full of birdlife. There are stiles leading into the marsh area, but they are of no relevance to you. Keep on the path with the fence on the right. In this manner you will pass through a few fields, between which there are stiles, all in good order and all obvious. A track goes off to the right, passing through a gate and over the stream. Though this may seem inviting, your way still lies onward, not through the gate.

The path now runs on top of a terrace, with the stream and marsh below on the right. Go over a stile in the fence ahead and keep close company with the fence on the right until a track is reached, trailing in from the right. Follow the track through the field, heading generally towards the white house, which now comes into view ahead. This is Wyaston Grove, which you will pass later on in the walk. The track skirts the flanks of the hillside, through a gate and into another field. You then cut across the field, still on the track and still heading towards the white house, to reach a gate. This leads into a lane, which doubles as a water course, at least near the gate. Go up the lane to its junction with the tarred road near Wyaston Grove. At least this is a pleasant place name, unlike the other nearby name on the map which rejoices in the description ''The Hole''!

Wyaston Grove

At the T-junction turn right and walk up the hill, passing Wyaston Grove on your right. Where the road bends to the left, there is a footpath sign on the right and a stile which takes you into fields. Keep the fence on your right. Ignore the first stile, but go through the second one beside the gate. Turn left and continue to follow the fence to another gate in the field corner. There is no stile here, but the gate does open. Now turn right and follow the hedge down the field. Part way down the field the hedge on your right does a quick left and right kink. There is a gap in the hedge at this point and there is some evidence that walkers on this path use the gap – there is no stile. However, the OS map implies that you should continue down the field, still keeping the hedge on your right, until you reach a gate in the bottom corner. There is no stile here either and both routes eventually lead to the same spot.

Bear left at this point, heading towards the bare patch which you can see on the opposite hillside. There is a good view across to Copse Hill House and Osmaston Park. You will find there is no sign of a path underfoot, but you will eventually locate a footbridge at the bottom of the field, just to the left of the oak tree. The bridge spans Wyaston Brook and takes you into a thin strip of woodland. The path suddenly becomes obvious in the wood, but it twists and turns in a bewildering fashion, until it comes up against a fence. If you explore to the left along the fence you will find a stile and thus you emerge into parkland. The path now vanishes!

Climb the hill towards the patch of bare earth you saw earlier and continue to ascend to the corner of the fence which surrounds the plantation. There is a stile here on the left, but this is of no use to you. Carry straight on, keeping to the left of the solitary tree to reach a stile in the fence ahead. There is another stile to the left of the gate, but this should be ignored and you should follow the track alongside the new plantation. The track soon reaches another gate and thus joins the driveway to Copse Hill House, seen on the right. Go left along the driveway, but where it bears left towards the gate, look out for a stile on the right, in the fence. There is another thin belt of new planting here, through which a sketchy path winds to a further stile.

Once clear of the new trees, continue up the field, with the fence and hedge on the right. The map implies that the path should be on the opposite side of the fence and hedge, but this is clearly not the case. Nevertheless, the fence and hedge do seem to enclose a narrow track, which is completely impassable. The path sticks to the open field until the end of the metal fence is reached, where there is a stile on the right. Go through this and turn left, alongside the hedge.

By Caravan to Osmaston

At the end of the field there are an overgrown hedge and fence, with a gate in the corner. When this walk was reconnoitred, the gate was defended by another fence consisting of a single strand of barbed wire, further out into the field. This is obviously designed to prevent cattle getting close to the gate, beyond which is a caravan site, once the village polo field. The fence presents no great obstacle to an agile walker, but the quagmire by the gate is a different matter. Go through the gate and into the caravan site. Thread your way through the vans, heading for the far goal posts. In this manner you will locate the main entrance where there are a stile and gate. This leads out onto the road where you turn right to enter Osmaston Village, just near the pond. Now is the time to sample the dubious comforts of the horseshoe seat.

The Shoulder of Mutton

18: PALTERTON

The Route: Palterton – Hill Top Farm – Terrace Wood – Glapwell –Stoney Houghton – Water Lane – Roseland Wood – Birch Hill Plantation –Poulterwell Lane – Palterton

Distance: 5 miles (8km). Allow 2 hours excluding pub stop

Start: Lay by near allotments, just off Mansfield Road, Palterton. Grid reference: 478683

Map(s): OS 1:25000 Pathfinder Series No. 779 Mansfield North

How to get there:

By Public Transport: Monday to Saturday service from Bolsover and Mansfield. The bus stops outside The Harlequin.

By Car: A632 to Bolsover (Hillstown) or A617 to Glapwell, then follow signs to Palterton.

The Pub

The Harlequin at Palterton is a curious looking pub with its flat roofs. It is one of the least photogenic pubs the author has ever seen. However, it serves a grand pint of John Smiths beers and you can be assured of a friendly welcome. There is a family room as well as seats and a play area outside. Opening hours are 12noon – 2.30pm and 5pm – 11pm, Monday to Friday, Saturday 12noon – 11pm, Sunday 12noon – 3pm and 7.30pm – 10.30pm.

The Walk

Walk down the road from the car park to the Harlequin. There's no footpath until the bus stop is reached near the pub. At the road junction just by the pub, go right, along Main Street, into Palterton village.

A Limestone Village with a Grand View

The older buildings in the village are attractively constructed in lime-stone. However, this is not the same sort of limestone found in the Peak District, but is Magnesian limestone, a softer, more yellow rock.

Continue along the road to Elm Tree Farm. The road drops away abruptly down Rylah Lane, but you go left along a track with limestone outcrops. There is a tremendous view from here, westwards over the M1 to the hills of the Peak.

The track continues past Hill Top Farm, with its large limestone barn and asbestos roof – ripe for restoration. Go over the stile by the gate and into open fields. The track soon forks. Go straight on here, not down to the right. The track follows the wall round to the left, where there is the usual collection of farmyard junk. This is soon left behind and the path proceeds along an obvious terrace. Note the curious 'V'-shaped stones. Any offers as to their use?

Looking ahead along the valley you can see Hardwick Hall, formerly the property of the Dukes of Devonshire but now in the ownership of the National Trust.

Bluebells in Spring

The terrace path soon becomes a sunken lane, with a fence to the right. Just before a gate, leave the track and go left, following the fence up the hill. Ignore the next gate on the right. You may spot a stile in the left-hand corner of the field, but ignore this and continue to follow the fence as it kinks to the right to another stile. The path then follows the edge of the scarp. On the right is a narrow band of woodland, full of bluebells in Spring. At the electricity pylon there is a break in the woodland and a view westwards to Bramley Vale and Heath.

The woodland finishes and the path runs alongside a hedge to a track at the northern tip of Terrace Wood. Since leaving the last stile you have been in one field for over three quarters of a kilometre, very different from the tiny fields of the limestone peak.

Cross the track and go straight ahead, across the middle of the next field, heading towards the barn and the solitary tree. Depending on what is growing in this field you should soon see a hedge in which there is a gap marked by a post. The farmer who cultivates these fields deserves congratulations for the way in which he delineates the paths.

As you near the "solitary" tree, it resolves into two. Keep straight on, with the red brick barn to your left, to reach a stile between two houses. The path disgorges into the well kept estate road of Pinfold. Go left and

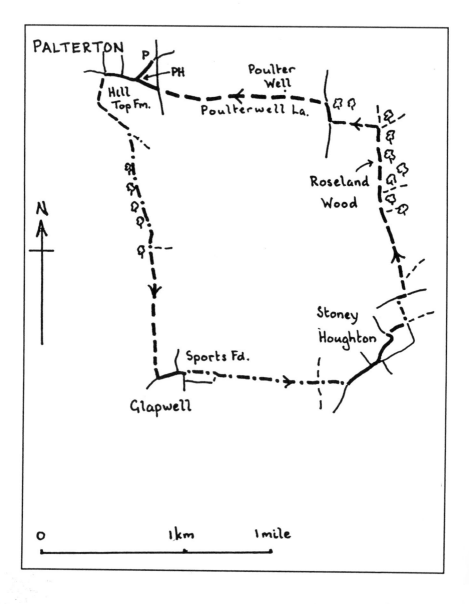

down to the road junction, then left again along Back Lane. This is Glapwell.

Of Limestone, Snowdrops and Glapwell

Despite appearances, Glapwell is an ancient village, being mentioned in Domesday Book as Glapewelle. In the 13th century the manor was held by the de Glapwells, who married into the Woodhouse family of Glapwell Hall. The hall was demolished in the 1960s and the site is now used as the village playing fields. The older properties in the village are again limestone. A great pity the newer ones couldn't have retained the traditional materials. Go past Snowdrop Farm on the left to reach the main road. Cross the road and bear right alongside the playing fields, which are where Glapwell Hall once stood. Where the road bends sharply to the right, the map shows the path continuing straight ahead. There is no sign of this, the route now being blocked by gardens of modern housing. However, at the bend there is a gate on the left into the playing fields. Go through this and turn right, keeping alongside the wall. A gateway leads onto the cricket ground, but still keep by the wall until, just before the pavilion, there is a black gate on the right. Go through the gate and immediately left through a stile into fields. (If there is a cricket match in progress, it would be better to avoid the playing fields by following the main road round the right-hand bend. Then take the next turning on the left, walk to the end of the cul de sac and there reach the black gate referred to earlier. The stile on the right leads into fields).

Hedge Hopping to Greer Lane

A sketchy path runs alongside the hedge, with a view to the left to Roseland Wood. Shortly, the hedge does a kink to the right, but the path goes straight on through a gap into another field. There is no stile. Still accompany the hedge though it's now on your right. The hedge kinks again, this time to the left and the path, true to form, keeps straight on through a stile-less gap. Carry on, this time with the hedge to your left and so reach the end of the field.

At the end of the field there is a gap in the hedge large enough for a lorry to drive through, so a mere walker should have no trouble. Go straight on, across the next field, heading to the right of the electricity pole. Again at the hedge, there is only a gap, but this leads into a narrow, overgrown track, known as Greer Lane. On the OS map this forms part of a remarkably straight north-south alignment of roads and tracks down this eastern fringe of the county. Cross Greer Lane and negotiate another gap in the hedge ahead to emerge into fields again. Stony Houghton is now in view and this is your next objective. Continue ahead, with the hedge on your right, (not as shown on the OS map), until at the end of the field there is a gateway on the right. Go through this and then immediately left, following the hedge to the inevitable gap leading onto Green Lane, which is a tarmac road. Here go left into the hamlet of Stony Houghton.

Stony Houghton

Pass Rock Cottage on the right and go straight ahead at the first road junction, where there is a bus stop. Cross the road and bear left at the next junction. Follow the lane down, past the telephone box, noting the outcrops of limestone on the right.

Where the lane turns left up to Houghton Bassett, go right, along the track. There is a seat here for those who are worn out, though you shouldn't be, for this is easy walking. Follow the track, which is known as Water Lane, presumably on account of the stream on the left. Pass the red roofed barn and go left between two barns, through the waymarked gate. Remember to close the gate behind you as there are likely to be cattle grazing in this next field.

Go up the field to a stile just to the left of the electricity pylon. Excellent waymarkers, pylons! Once over the stile, turn right and go along the lane for a short distance. Just past the pylon there is a signed track off to the left. This leads to a waymarked stile by a gate.

Carry on along this track until it forks. The right-hand fork is private and says so. Your route is straight on, along the signed and waymarked track towards Roseland Wood.

Roseland Wood

Keeping the hedge on your left, head for the gateway at the corner of Roseland Wood. The spire of Bolsover Church and the water tower at Hillstown can be seen ahead, with Palterton more to the left. Keep straight on at the gateway at the end of the wood, to another waymarked gate by a pylon. Just beyond this gateway the track forks, one going off into the wood, the other carrying straight on. Both are waymarked, which makes for confusion. Go straight on, keeping the wood on your right and pass through two more gateways, descending now towards Birch Hill Plantation.

Scarcliffe village is now in view ahead, but your route goes left at the end of the next field, where the path splits three ways. Proceed to the left, keeping the hedge and Birch Hill Plantation to the right. The path soon brings you to the old Mansfield – Rotherham road, where you negotiate a stile by a gate and turn right.

Poulterwell Lane

Follow the road as it descends to cross a culvert. Then ascend slightly until you reach a track on the left, signed as a public bridleway. This is Poulterwell Lane and it runs unerringly back to Palterton. The map shows the Poulter Well on the right-hand side of the lane, about 300 metres from the junction with the road. However, apart from a cluster of willow trees and an obviously wet patch, there is nothing to be seen. Poulterwell Lane is a lovely green road, sunken in places, with all sorts of trees and shrubs in the banks and hedges. It is a joy to walk along. Soon it emerges on the "new" Mansfield Road, opposite Palterton Main Street. The Harlequin lies straight ahead, less than 200 metres away.

19: REPTON

The Route: Repton – Monsom Lane – Repton Cemetery – Old Trent Water –Twyford (almost) – Foremark – Milton – Repton

Distance: 5.6 miles (9km)

Start: Car park on Burton Road, Repton Grid reference: 303269

Map(s): OS 1:25000 Pathfinder Series No. 852, Burton on Trent

How to get there:

By Public Transport: Daily bus services from Derby and Burton on Trent.

By Car: B5008 from Burton on Trent passes the car park. Repton is signed off the A38 and the car park is signed from the cross in the centre of the town.

The Pub

The Swan Inn, situated on the main street in Milton, is an excellent local pub, serving Marstons beers and Murphy's Stout. Like many others in

The Swan

this book, the pub is CAMRA listed. The author can vouch for the friendliness of the welcome and the joy of the real fire in the depths of winter. In summer, or if you're a masochist, there's seating outside. Opening hours are 12.00noon – 2.30pm and 7.00pm – 11.00pm on Monday to Friday, 12.00noon – 3.00pm and 6.30pm – 11.00pm on Saturday, 12.00noon – 3.00pm and 7.00pm –10.30pm on Sundays. Food is served at lunchtimes and evenings except on Mondays. Before you get too carried away with the Pedigree, bear in mind there are no bus services back to Repton.

The Walk

From the car park, turn right and walk into the centre of the town, passing the Red Lion *en route*. There is a fine thatched cottage opposite the car park and the graceful spire of the church can be seen above the surrounding roof tops.

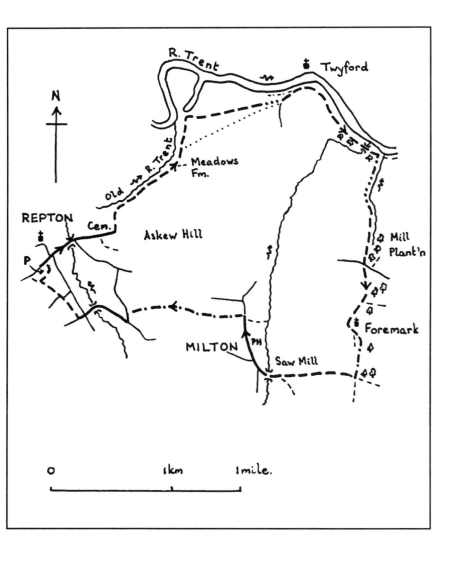

Repton

Repton is a fine old town and well worth an hour or two of your time. The church is particularly fine, especially the crypt, where the bodies of the Saxon kings of Mercia were buried in the 7th century. The church became a place of pilgrimage until destroyed by the Danes in 875. Remarkably, the crypt survived and became the focus of a rebuilt church in the 10th century. A priory was founded in 1172 and continued on the site until the Dissolution of the Monasteries by Henry VIII. After that the priory buildings were effectively plundered for stone, but the crypt was "lost" under the rubble until an 18th century grave-digger, going about his daily tasks, fell through the roof and rediscovered the site. The famous public school of Repton, utilises the foundations of the Priory church. According to Bede, the cross in the centre of the town is supposed to mark the spot where Christianity was first preached in the Midlands in 653. The first Repton church and monastery were founded shortly afterwards. The present church is still dedicated to St Wystan, a Mercian prince and martyr. It is noted for its superb spire. There is the tale told of a steeplejack, Joseph Barton, who in 1804, having finished his repairs to the spire, climbed to the top of the ball at the very pinnacle. In his delight he dropped the connecting rope, but was saved by the courage of his young daughter who climbed the ladders on the outside of the steeple and, 200 feet above ground calmly retrieved the rope and threw it up to her father. Leave time in your day to explore the town if you can.

At the old cross, go across the High Street and down a narrow alleyway to the right of Repton Furnishing. This descends to the Boot Inn and another road. Continue straight ahead, soon joining the main road down from the cross. Note the Priory Mill arch, now incorporated into the wall on your left. Soon, the main road swings to the right and a narrow lane goes straight on, signed as a No Through Road. This is Monsom Lane. Follow the lane past the houses, ignoring the footpath sign on the right. At the top of the lane is Repton Cemetery on the left. The lane now degenerates into a track and swings left just past the cemetery.

Beside the Old Trent Water

The well-defined track now begins to descend towards the valley bottom. There is a wide view from this point, right across the Trent Valley to the higher hills of the southern Peak District. Willington Power Station is prominent, but some people find the cooling towers graceful and the ever-changing patterns of the steam attractive. Repton church spire can be seen to the left. At the bottom of the "hill", the track runs alongside a narrow stream. The map proclaims this as the Old Trent Water. Hard to believe that this tiny trickle was once the mighty Trent.

Carry on along the track with the willow lined stream to the left. The land is flat and the views constrained, but the walking is very easy and the profusion of flowers and birdlife is ample compensation. At the first fork in the track, keep left, ignoring the route to Meadows Farm. Similarly at the second fork, again keep left, passing through the gate or stile, whichever is the easier. The map shows a path diverging right here, but there is no sign of it on the ground. Better by far to continue along the track. The spire of Twyford church can be seen to the right, peeping up above the trees.

At the next gate and stile, the stream on the left suddenly broadens out. The main Trent river is only 100 metres away but it can scarcely be seen apart from the fringing willows. Here the track ceases, its main use seems to be to enable fishermen to drive to this spot for a days quiet enjoyment. Turn right and carry on alongside the hedge to the next gateway. Keeping alongside the left-hand hedge this time, follow the raised path through a series of stiles and gates, always heading towards Twyford church. Eventually you arrive in a field with no hedge on the left. Here the path cuts straight across to a gate and stile in the far hedge. A low mound along the left-hand edge of the field marks the Trent bank. At the gate and stile go left along the hedged track, but not into the fishermen's car park.

Twyford, So Near Yet So Far

Pass through another gate and stile with a plethora of angling notices. You are now very close to the Trent, but it still cannot be seen. However, Twyford can be seen close nearby, while closer still is a large wooden post. On examining this post more closely you will discover that it has a counterpart on the opposite side of the river. It has a large hook embedded near the top and was clearly once used for a chain or rope ferry. If you had envisaged popping into Twyford for a bit of sightseeing, you will be sadly disappointed, as there is neither bridge nor ferry. This is a pity, for Twyford has a 14th century church with some fine memorials to the Harpur family.

Return to the track, which bears right, away from the river again to pass through a gateway. Twyford Hall can be seen to the left, on the waters edge, looking in a sorry state. The map shows a footpath proceeding in a straight line across these next fields, but it does not exist in practice.

Follow the well blazed track, for which you can thank the fishermen again. The river soon comes close again on the left and, perhaps surprisingly there is a variety of bird life using it. Various gulls, ducks and a merganser were seen when the walk was being tested.

Continue along the track until it ends at a car park in a clump of willow scrub. A stile at the far end of the car park takes you onto a narrow riverside path, well trodden but totally at variance to the right of way shown on the map. This winds through the willows to a bridge over a tributary stream. Do not cross the bridge, but go right, over the stile in the fence, onto what is shown on the map as a right of way. There is some doubt as to the exact location of the right of way, which seems to dodge about from one side of the hedge to the other according to the map. Ignoring this, walk up the field with the hedge on your left, leaving the river behind. There is one very swampy stretch where it is impossible to stick close to the hedge, but apart from this there are no problems. At the end of the field, go through the gate or over the stile into a rough and muddy lane. Follow the lane at it rises steadily towards Foremark church, which can be seen ahead. Part way along the lane, a glance left will reveal the rock outcrops of Anchor Church. The track crosses a bridge and soon joins the road. At this point you can either carry and complete this Repton walk, or you can pick up the route of the Stanton by Bridge walk and extend the circuit to 12 miles.

Foremark, No Village; Just a Church, A School and A Farm

Cross over the road and head off up the track signed as the heavy goods vehicle route to Repton School and the access to Home Farm. There is no indication that this is a public footpath, other than your map. The track is rough underfoot, not being helped by the passage of lorries. As you gently ascend towards the church, you will see Foremark Hall on the left, now part of the Repton School complex. The hall was built to the design of the Warwick architect, Hiorne, for Sir Robert Burdett. It was finished in 1762. Go past the driveway on the left, which leads to the school. The track now reaches Foremark church, a curiously squat building, heavily shaded by yew trees. The church was built in 1662 in what is known to devotees of church architecture as Late Perpendicular style. It contains some excellent old woodwork, including a rood screen, box pews and a three-decker pulpit.

There is a good view back over the Vale of Trent from here, with Willington Power Station being particularly prominent. At the church the track forks. Keep right and follow the track as it bends round to the left to reach Home Farm. Go through the gateway, passing the big barn on the right. Just beyond the barn the track forks again. Your route lies straight on, dipping into the old part of the farmyard, then turning right to run between the farm buildings. At the end of the buildings there are a gate and stile and you are out into fields again.

Once in the field, follow the track up the shallow valley to the gateway at the top, just to the right of the wood. The Stanton walk joins here, having come through the wood. Ignore both the stile into the wood and the gateway ahead. Instead, turn right and follow the top hedge of the field to reach a gate in the far corner, near the holly bush. It will now be obvious that you have just completed two sides of a triangle! Go through the gate into a hedged green lane and follow this until you reach the next gate. Beyond this point, the hedge on the left has many gaps in it and eventually gives out completely. The main track is sunken, very muddy and churned up, so walkers seem to use a well-beaten path on the left. This is accessed by the first gap in the hedge. Continue in this manner above the quagmire, with Milton in view ahead and to the right.

Rejoin the track where it ceases to be muddy, just before the barn. Follow the track down, through the gate and skirt Saw Mills Farm, with its barking, but chained dog. Cross the stream and continue along the track as it bears right. At the fork, keep right, passing the white house and ascending to meet the main road.

Milton

Follow the road into Milton, soon reaching the Swan Inn on the right-hand side. There is quite a lot of development going on in the village, but equally there is a fair amount of dereliction. Milton is predominantly an agricultural village, though now in the throes of "invasion" by commuters. Oddly for a place of this size, it has neither church nor any form of public transport. The estate passed to the Burdett family in 1602 and they made their home at Foremark. The villagers therefore have to rely on Foremark church for their C of E version of spiritual welfare. Ironically, much of the land in the area is now in the ownership of the Church Commissioners.

On leaving the pub, cross the road and go right. Look out for two footpath signs on the opposite side of the road. One points into fields. The other points across the road to a gateway into a farmyard. This is your route, so you should turn left here. Bear right across the farmyard, to pass underneath the covered way. The farm has a fine range of outbuildings, clustered round the courtyard. All now seem disused and in a state of disrepair. A great shame. The "path" goes across a further concreted yard, with more derelict buildings on either side. At the far end of the yard there is a stile and the path becomes a narrow green lane. A further stile at the end of the lane, takes you out into open fields again.

Keep the hedge to your left through this field. Willington Power Station can be seen away to the right, while Repton church spire is also in view. Where the hedge does a sharp kink to the left, the path carries straight on across the field, heading for the spire. At the far side of the field is a stile and the well blazed path continues across the next field to reach a stile and plank bridge over a ditch.

The Back Way into Repton

The route bears to the left of the new houses to reach another stile. Beyond the next stile, the path dips towards Repton. Tethered horses in this field might lead to deviations from the true right of way, but the exit lies to the right of the paling fence opposite. A narrow alleyway leads between fences down to the road. Here go left to reach a T-junction. At the T-junction go right and descend the road. The map shows a path going off to the right, but the author defies you to find any trace of it. At the bottom of the hill the road bends to the left and crosses the stream. The Wesleyan Reform Church is on the left. Soon you reach a cross roads. Go straight across, locating a footpath sign which points to the Burton Road. Continue along the road for about 100 metres, then, just beyond the last building on the right, go right, along a narrow path, with woodland on the left and gardens on the right.

Ignore gates and paths to the right, most of which simply lead into private gardens. Follow the path until it descends a flight of steps to reach a road. Cross the road and go left and then at once right, along the lane signed as a private road. It is a public footpath. Soon the lane forks three ways. Your route is the centre of the three, straight on between the posts, passing some of the many buildings belonging to the famous Repton School on the left. When you reach the white cones, go right, taking care not to go down the private drive instead of the narrow footpath. The path is hemmed in on either side by fence and hedge but it takes you unerringly to your destination. At one point only can you go wrong, for the path forks. Go left at the fork and end up back on the Burton Road alongside the Red Lion. The car park lies just to the left.

20: ROSLISTON

The Route: Rosliston – Caldwell – Longlands Farm – Blakehall Farm –Longfurlong Farm – Coton in the Elms – Rosliston

Distance: 3.9 miles (6.25km)

Start: Grid reference: 243166. Rough layby on the Rosliston to Coton road

Map(s): OS 1:25000 Pathfinder Series No. 873 Ashby de la Zouch

How to get there:

By Public Transport: There is a Monday to Saturday service from Burton on Trent and Swadlincote to Rosliston and Coton.

By Car: From the A38 follow the signs to Walton on Trent, then the signs to Rosliston. From the A444 follow the signs to Linton, then the signs for Rosliston. In Rosliston take the lane signposted to Coton to reach the parking spot, just past the new houses.

The Pub

The pub is the Royal Oak at Caldwell, or Cauldwell as it is shown on the map. The Royal Oak is a lively village local serving Marston's beers. It has two main rooms, the low beamed public bar being the one for walkers. Dirty boots don't seem to be a problem here, but take your plastic bags just in case. Food is served lunchtimes and evenings and families are welcomed. There is a beer garden round the back of the pub.

The Walk

From the parking place on Coton Lane, walk back towards the new houses. Turn right, into the field, just before the first house. Follow the left-hand hedge to the end of the field and go straight on, over a stile and into a new housing estate. Where the estate road swings left, go straight on following the sign to Yew Tree Gardens. This tarred track

soon brings you out onto the main road in Rosliston. The village is
referred to in Domesday Book as "Redlauseton" and at that time boasted
a church. The present building however is much newer, having been
rebuilt and extended in the early 19th century. The spire, which is the
most obvious feature, is a 14th century survival. Those of the Methodist
persuasion were once catered for by a chapel next to the Plough Inn, but
unlike the situation at Dale Abbey, there is no record of a connecting

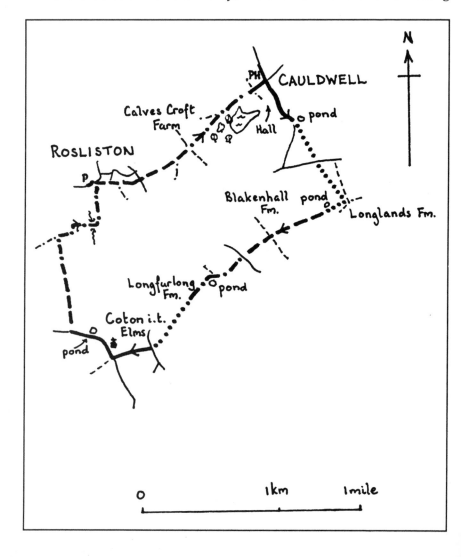

door. The village is mainly agricultural, though now with a strong leavening of commuters. As a measure of the criminal nature of the inhabitants, the most celebrated theft took place in 1859, when quantities of onions and beans were stolen. The culprit has never been apprehended, nor were the stolen goods recovered.

Cross the road and take the track on the opposite side, which is signed to Caldwell. This passes the playground on the left before reaching open fields. The water tower at Winshill, near Burton is seen ahead and to the left. More prominent still is Drakelow Power Station. At this distance it contrives to look impressive, not intimidating. The track soon swings away to the left, heading for Calves Croft Farm. Carry straight on here, through a gap in the hedge ahead, not to the right, and continue down the field with the hedge to your right.

Caldwell Village

The trees of Caldwell Covert are soon encountered on the right, but the path does not enter the woodland, preferring to skirt round it on the left. In this fashion you soon reach a culverted stream and a stile. There is evidence that some previous visitors have deviated from the path and entered the wood, but this is not your route. Carry on alongside the wood, then where the woodland fence bears away to the right, continue across the field, heading to the left of Caldwell church. A track joins from the right and you follow this to a muddy gateway to the left of the church. Here you join Church Lane. The church is dedicated to St Giles and contains some remnants of Saxon and Norman buildings. Inevitably, the village was recorded in Domesday Book.

Follow the lane down to the cross roads, noting the ingenious use of the telephone pole as a netball goal. At the crossroads, go left to the pub.

On leaving the pub, retrace your steps to the crossroads and this time, carry straight on. The big house on the right is Caldwell Hall, built in 1678, though some parts are newer. Curiously, the Hall was surrounded by a moat, cut out of solid rock and the yard in front of the hall is also bed-rock. Before the Reformation, the manor was held by Burton Abbey, whose members were among the first of the Burton brewing interests. The owners of the estate in the 18th century were the Evans family, who were also involved in the Burton brewing industry. One of their daughters married into the Worthingtons, another brewery family. This tiny village thus has its place in the history of the British brewery industry.

Follow the road as it bends first to the left and then to the right. At the right-hand bend, leave the road, bearing left through a gate into fields. There is a pond on the left, populated by noisy geese, but fortunately they don't seem to be interested in walkers. In the field bear right, heading towards the right-hand side of the house. There is no obvious path in this field, and some of the boundaries shown on the map have been grubbed out. Still heading towards the house, you will see a sign post in the hedge ahead and this marks the presence of a stile. The stile is defended by an electric fence, but with a hop, step and a jump, you are taken onto the Linton – Rosliston road. Go straight across to another stile and thus back into fields again.

An Annoying Route

The path is shown on the map as heading for Longlands Farm, which is the house you were using as a marker in the previous field. There is again no obvious path in this field but you should make towards the left hand end of the house. When you reach the far corner of the field, by the gate, turn right. Do not go through the gate, but keep alongside the fence, past the bungalow. Struggle through a boggy area at the far corner of the field to reach a gate, just to the left of the pond. It will be obvious to all but the most incompetent map reader, that you have just gone along two sides of a triangle and that a quicker route exists to this same spot. However, you can console yourself with the virtuous thought that at least you followed the right of way!

Go through the gate and straight across the next field, heading to the left of the barn. Field boundaries have been removed here with great gusto, and the field you are in bears no resemblance to that shown on the map. However, the farmer is a credit to his calling in that the path is clearly marked right across the field. You pass to the left of Blakehall Farm, by the two trees in mid field. There is a good view across to the frontage of Caldwell Hall from this point. Ahead is the spire of Coton church and this serves as a good marker for quite a distance. Carry straight on towards the church, ignoring paths left and right. Eventually you will reach the end of this big field and emerge onto a lane, having scrambled over a stile.

Go over the lane and over the stile (of sorts) opposite. Ignore the gateway just on the right and go over the stile ahead. The path now runs alongside the right-hand edge of the field. As the author was checking out this walk, he was regularly ducking in the mistaken belief that he was being shot at. The explosions you hear turn out to be bird scarers and should not alarm you at all. At the end of the field there is a gate in the right-hand corner. The map shows the path diverging right just before the gate and there is a stile of dubious nature in the hedge on the right, easily missed. Most walkers seem to use the gate. Go through the gate and onto the area of tipped ground. Keep alongside the right-hand fence for a short distance, then bear left across the tipped area to reach a stile, which is waymarked by a brick wedged in a tree stump!

Pond Blocks Path!

Keep alongside the hedge on the left. Just over the hedge, there is a large pond, which bears little resemblance to that shown on the map. It may have been caused by subsidence, but is now being infilled. Where the hedge kinks to the left, carry straight on, heading for the gate, waymarked by a large yellow footprint. There is also a stile at this point and a culverted stream. In the next field, Coton church spire, which has served well as a long distance waymark, now proves unreliable. You need to bear to the left of the spire, finally discovering a "stile" to the left of the brick built garages. This leads onto the garage access drive and then onto the main road.

Coton in The Elms

Go straight across the road and up Elms Road, to the Shoulder of Mutton pub. Here, at the T-junction, go right and shortly pass the church on your right. This is a relatively modern structure, dating only from 1846. It replaced an earlier building which stood behind the Shoulder of Mutton Inn. Oddly, the bells from the original church were removed and taken to nearby Lullington, where they are still rung. The village is one of many in this book which can be traced back to that earlier work of research, Domesday Book. Then it was called "Cotune". Of the elms in the village name there is now no sign. They have all succumbed to Dutch Elm disease, though all roads in the village used to have some examples at one time. Keep on along the road, noting the decorated tiled roof of the house on the right, just past Church Close.

Return to Rosliston

You soon leave Coton with no Elms behind and continue along the lane. There is no footway, but fortunately there is not much traffic either. Go past the derestriction signs and the pond on the right, then, just past the village nameplate sign, there is a gateway and footpath sign on your right. Go right here, along the track through the fields, with Drakelow Power Station in all its glory straight ahead. Rosliston church spire is also in view, so you know that the end of the walk is nigh. Keep the hedge on your left and follow the track through a gateway into another field. Part way along this field, there is a gateway to the left. This you should ignore. There is also a gateway ahead, where the hedge does a slight kink. The track appears to pass through this gateway into the field with the pylon in it, but this is not the route of the path. The path steers to the right of the gate, continuing to keep the hedge to the left. In this manner you will reach the end of the field, where there are a stile and a bridge, well hidden in the corner. Turn your back on these temptations and go right, alongside the hedge, to the far corner of the field, where there is an even better hidden bridge, by an oak tree. Cross the brook and go up the bank, following the left-hand hedge. Where the hedge kinks left then right, the map shows the right of way doing the same. Evidence on the ground suggests that users cut the corner, heading straight for the stile by the gate in the top left-hand corner of the field.

At the gate and stile, go left by the fence to reach a muddy stile by the pond. Rosliston is now in view ahead. Still keep by the left-hand hedge and follow it round to the gap by the new houses, which is where the walk began.

21: SHARDLOW

The Route: Shardlow Car Park – Trent and Mersey Canal – Derwent Mouth/Long Horse Bridge – Trent Bank – Crowder's Eaves – Cavendish Bridge –Shardlow Canal Port – Shardlow Car Park

Distance: 3.25 miles (5km)

Start: Public car park off Great Wilne road. Grid reference: 445303

Map(s): OS 1:25000 Pathfinder Series Nos. 833, Nottingham SW and 853, Loughborough' North

How to get there:

By Public Transport: Daily bus service from Derby, Loughborough' and Leicester.

By Car: A6 to Shardlow then follow sign for Great Wilne, to reach the car park.

The Pub

The pub is the New Inn, Shardlow, a fine canal-side hostelry serving Bass beers. It is open all day except Sundays and welcomes walkers and families. It has the added attraction of open fires, ideal on a cold day. Food is served at lunchtimes and evenings. The internal arrangement is a little odd, there being one big bar arranged like a peninsular to give three serving areas in one room. Also unusual is the collection of ties which are displayed at the bar. Investigations were rebuffed, but dark hints were dropped that these were souvenirs from the landlady's past conquests. At this point the author hurriedly retreated.

The Walk

This is a short and easy walk. The greatest ascent is the climb from the canal bank up onto the bridge. Having said that, it is an unusual and interesting stroll alongside one of our oldest canals and visiting a fine inland port of eighteenth century vintage.

Traffic Lights on The Canal!

From the car park turn right along the Gt. Wilne road and follow the
road until you reach the bridge over the Trent and Mersey Canal. From
the top of the bridge you can see, to the left, the canal port of Shardlow,
which grew up around the T&M. You can also see the New Inn and the
adjacent Marstons pub, The Malt Shovel. Despite the shortness of the
walk, there's no shortage of pubs en route, there being five in all. Do not
go over the bridge at this stage, unless you want a pre walk jar, but
remember you've got to walk alongside a canal and river. Better save the
drink until afterwards. Descend to the towpath and follow this away
from the pubs and out into countryside. The lie of the land is flat, but
not without interest. Radcliffe on Soar Power Station can be seen ahead
and then to your surprise there is a set of traffic lights guarding a flood
lock on the canal.

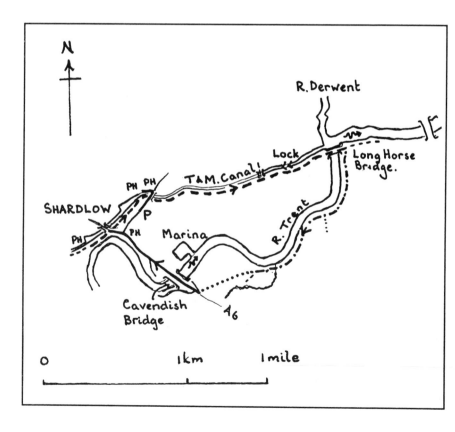

Long Horse Bridge, The Mouth of The Derwent

An easy stroll along the towpath follows. Bridge number one is soon reached and then shortly afterwards you arrive at Derwent Mouth Lock, the last (or first) lock on the canal. If there is a boat coming through stop for a while and watch, or better still, offer to help in swinging the heavy gates. This is not a narrow boat canal, but was built to take Trent barges, so the gates take some effort. Beyond the lock the "canal" becomes steadily more river-like until you reach a green direction sign, similar to those you get on a class A road. This shows the proximity of the junction with the Trent and Derwent. The towpath now ascends Long Horse Bridge. From the top of this you can see the Derwent mouth and the T&M, while underneath and then to the right, flows the Trent itself. At one stage all these routes were navigable and three still are, but the Derwent Navigation has fallen into disuse. The introduction mentioned that Derbyshire had everything except a coastline. This is the nearest you will get to coastal features, but you could be forgiven for thinking you were very close to the sea when you spot Cormorants fishing, to say nothing of the multitude of Gulls.

Carry on over the bridge, then down through a gap in the thorns on the right of the towpath, to pick up a narrow path alongside the Trent. Head upstream, with the river on your right and the gravel pits on the left. Where the extraction of gravel has ceased the water rapidly fills the space created and the areas are rapidly colonised by water plants and wildfowl. Even on some working pits there are ducks of various descriptions. On the river there are Great Crested Grebes, Mute Swans, plus the occasional boat. The large bowstring bridge seen spanning the river,if you look back and to the right, carries the Derwent Aqueduct over the Trent en route to Leicester.

Crowder's Eaves

Continue along the narrow path, which keeps company with the river on the right. There are occasional waymarks on willow trees, but these are not really necessary. The map shows a path turning off to the left near Crowder's Eaves, but there's no sign of it on the ground so no possibility of confusion. You pass through the remains of a couple of fences and then reach a derelict white gate of curious design. Here a track goes left, but you keep straight on alongside the river. Look out for an orange way marker, just before the path crosses a gravel bank. Again there is a curiously shaped white gate, probably a remnant of the old towing path when the Trent Navigation stretched all the way up to Burton.

Still keeping by the river, ignore the obvious track bearing left towards Donnington Power Station and head instead for the white house, just to the left of the maltings. There is no clear path at this point, but the white house is as good a waymarker as you will get. The route passes through a gap in the hedge, moving steadily away from the river bank. Carry on across the field and locate a stile just to the left of the white house. The ascent of the stile and the subsequent climb up onto the A6 represents the longest uphill section of the walk.

At the A6 go right, keeping on the right-hand side of the road over the Cavendish Bridge. The Shardlow Marina is on the right and this represents the current limit of navigation on the river. Just over the bridge, on the left-hand side of the road, is a monument which gives details of the tolls charged on the original bridge. The tolls had to be the same as those charged on the former rope ferry, so there was a maximum fare of two shillings and six pence, (12.5p), which in 1758 was a considerable sum. The original bridge was swept away in 1947. If you do cross the road at this point, take care and don't step on the crocuses. Continue along the A6, passing the Navigation Inn on the right and so coming to the road signed to Great Wilne. The car park lies just down to the right, but you are strongly recommended to continue along the A6, crossing over now, until you reach the bridge over the T&M canal. You will notice how close the canal is to the river at this point. The original idea was to finish the canal here, but the route was later extended to finish at Derwent mouth as you have seen.

Shardlow

Despite the canal influence, Shardlow is actually an ancient settlement. It is recorded in Domesday as Serdelaw and was then in the ownership of Chester Abbey. Its original reason for existence was the crossing of the Trent and the two roads from Derby to Loughborough and from Aston to Wilne. The Derby to Loughborough' road was turnpiked in 1738, but the Trent was crossed by a ferry until 1760, when the Cavendish Bridge was built. The ferry was rope worked. From 1788 to 1841 the village grew rapidly because of the canal trade. The remaining canal buildings were declared a conservation area in 1978. The wealth that the canal brought is dramatically shown by the fine buildings in the port area and its immediate surroundings.

At the canal bridge, go left and descend to the towpath by the old Salt Warehouse. Thus you reach the finely preserved canal port. On the opposite side of the cut is the Clock Warehouse, now beautifully converted into a pub and restaurant known as Hoskin's Wharf. It serves Wadworths beers and is open from 12noon – 2.30pm and 7pm – 10pm on seven days a week. It is not easily reached from the towpath, access only being possible by walking across the lock gates. However it is worth a look and the lock is good fun too. Retrace your steps to the Salt Warehouse, then continue along the towpath, under the A6. There are more canal basins and warehouses on the far side of the bridge, giving some idea of how important this place was in the heyday of canals.

Continue along the towpath, noting the fine milepost on the right. The canal swings to the left and the Malt Shovel comes into view, soon followed by the New Inn and bridge number two. Leave the towpath just before the bridge and ascend to the road, either going left to the pub, or right, to the car park.

22: SHIPLEY PARK (MAPPERLEY)

The Route: Shipley Park – Mapperley Car park – Mapperley Wood –Mapperley village – Cotgreave – Two Elms – Shipley Country Park – Mapperley Car Park

Distance: 4 miles (6.5km)

Start: Mapperley Car Park, Shipley Country Park Grid reference: 434437

Map(s): OS 1:25000 Pathfinder Series No. 812 Nottingham North and Ilkeston

How to get there:

By Public Transport: Monday to Saturday service from Derby, Ilkeston and Mansfield to Mapperley village.

By Car: From the A609 at West Hallam, follow the signs for Mapperley and Shipley Park. In Mapperley village go straight on into the country park. The car park is on the left, just over the dam.

The Pub

The Old Black Horse is now the only pub in Mapperley village. It is only 300 metres from the Country Park if you happen to be a crow, but not if you are using this book. The beers sold are Hardy Hansons (Kimberley) Ales and a fine pint you'll get too. The pub has a fascinating history. It was renovated in a mock half-timbered style in the late 19th, early 20th century. One former landlord rejoiced in the surname "Beer", and was an avid collector of odds and ends, with which he decorated the pub. No singing was allowed, but an early form of juke box was installed for entertainment. He also installed electric lighting, using his own generator, in the late 1890s. Nowadays the pub serves as an excellent village local and a haven for visitors to the Country Park. Opening hours are 12.00noon – 3.00pm and 7.00pm – 11.00pm, Monday to Friday, 11.00am –3.00pm and 7.00pm – 11.00pm on Saturday, 12.00noon – 3.00pm and 7.00pm –10.30pm on Sundays. Bar snacks are available at lunchtimes, Monday to Saturday, with Sunday lunches by prior arrangement. There is a large garden area.

The Walk

From the car park, go down to the information point and the lake side. Go left alongside the lake, taking care to step over the rods and lines of anglers. When you reach the road cross over and go down the track opposite, which leads along the northern edge of Mapperley Wood. This is a heavily used path and can be very muddy. After skirting the wood for some time, the path eventually swings right and enters the trees. Here there is a bridge over the stream. Signs to the right proclaim that this is a wildlife reserve, so don't wander off the path please. After another bridge, the path emerges from the wood and climbs steadily.

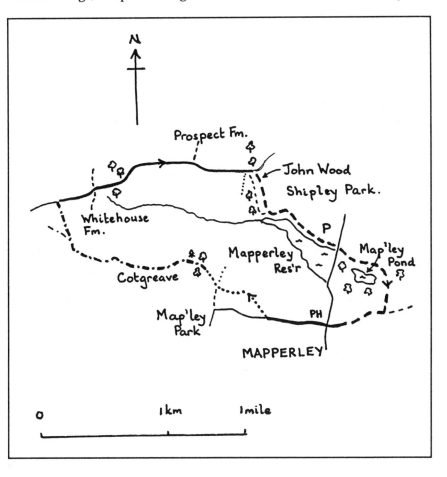

Ignore the Screams

You will hear occasional screams coming from your left. Sometimes it seems that whole groups of people are being murdered. However, before you rush for the nearest phone or sprint back to your car for safety, you will be relieved to learn that these are the normal noises associated with people enjoying themselves at the American Adventure Park. As your path rises, you will see the Adventure Park away to the left.

At the T-junction go right, along the track to Mapperley village. It is signed, but this is scarcely necessary as you can see the village ahead anyhow. The village is approached on a raised causeway and there is a good view back from here, over Ilkeston and the Erewash valley into Nottinghamshire.

As the first houses are reached, the track becomes a proper street, grandly named Coronation Road. At the cross roads in the centre of the village, go straight on to reach the Old Black Horse pub.

Mapperley

The name Mapperley is said to derive from the proliferation of maple trees, but whether that is true or not, the village is ancient. There was a charter of 1267 granting the right to hold an annual fair and market. Usually the church is the oldest building, but Mapperley's church was only built in 1851 and was closed in 1964 because of colliery subsidence. Happily it is now restored. The colliery which caused the problem closed in 1966 and the site has now been well and truly landscaped.

On leaving the pub, turn right and carry straight on along the road, passing the farm on the left and the playground on the right. Pass the unusual timber houses, appropriately called The Limes and then seek out a gate and stile on the right. This boasts both a signpost and a waymarker. In the field bear diagonally left, ignoring the more obvious track to the right. Marlpool church is in view to the right, perched on its hilltop. The exit stile from this field is in the corner by the gate. Then follow the right-hand hedge cum fence to reach a double stile. This is not as shown on the map. There have been one or two changes round here since the colliery closed!

A plank bridge leads over a ditch onto a track. The map shows another pub just to the left at Mapperley Park. It doesn't exist. Turn right at the track and go through the gate/stile then go left over another stile into a wet and muddy field. Go straight across the middle of the field to reach a stile in the middle of the far boundary fence. Beyond this stile is an area of new planting, covering the former Mapperley Colliery site. Footpaths have been altered here with gay abandon, so take care. A narrow path winds through the new trees and eventually reaches a stile on the far side. This gives out onto a track. Here go right. Where the trees cease a very wide view opens up to the north. A gate is soon reached, with an accompanying quagmire. The track continues to another gate with a stile alongside. Again the ground is very wet and muddy. The map shows this as Cotgreave, but of this there is no sign.

Carry straight on alongside the left-hand hedge to reach a stile in the far corner of the field. This is a wet and muddy stretch, with much evidence of new fences and post-colliery land restoration. Once over the stile, follow the fence on the right alongside the new plantation. There is a stile by the oak tree, one of the few old features in this otherwise new landscape. Ignore the gate ahead and go along the path to the right, through the sloe bushes, to reach a stile. Now keep the hedge on your left, stick to the marginally drier raised causeway and arrive at a stile by another gate and oak tree. Keep straight on, follow the left-hand hedge, which bears right at the end of the field, and arrive at a gate and stile. There is a view left over Smalley towards Horsley Woodhouse.

Ignore the path diverging left across the field towards Smalley and instead carry on alongside the right-hand hedge to a stile that deposits you on a rough road. Turn right here, along the track. The map shows that there is a footpath running parallel to the track on the left-hand side. This was once a common way of separating pedestrian traffic from horse drawn vehicles, but you will look in vain for any sign of the path in this instance. Follow the rough road instead.

When is an Elm not an Elm?

Whitehouse Farm is passed on the right, an odd looking place with decorative brickwork and leaning chimneys. Go straight on, through the gateway, noting the well on the left-hand side. The lane now passes through a short stretch of beech/oak woodland. Very pleasant and full of bird life. Beyond the wood, you can see Ilkeston to your right. Shortly you will pass Two Elms bungalow on the right. Despite the name, there are four trees, of which two are oaks and the others appear to be beech!

Soon the lane forks. Keep to the right-hand route. That to the left only leads to Prospect Farm. Marlpool and Heanor are now in view to the left. The lane now dips towards the stream and there is a footpath sign on the right. Ignore this and proceed past the three tonne weight limit sign and the sign telling you that you are entering Shipley Country Park.

Shipley and The Miller-Mundys

The modernity of the country park belies the history of Shipley. It was recorded as a manor before Domesday. The Millers, who held the manor, married into the Mundy family from Allestree. The Miller-Mundy family then held the manor from 1729 to 1920, during which time the mineral wealth of the area was greatly exploited. Shipley Hall was demolished in 1942, having fallen victim to mining subsidence. In 1976, Derbyshire County Council acquired the 900 acre estate, including 25 houses and farms. Six hundred acres were turned into Shipley Country Park.

Ignore the path leading off to the right and carry on over the culvert. Bear right by the gate, following the sign to Mapperley Reservoir. The path twists and turns into John Wood with the stream on the right. Your path is soon joined from the right by another route. Continue ahead, soon coming alongside the reservoir. There is a choice of routes here, either the bridleway or the lakeside footpath. If you are in a hurry, the bridleway is better, but scenically the lakeside path is to be preferred. Either way, you will eventually arrive back at the car park.

23: SHORT HEATH (OVERSEAL)

The Route: Short Heath – Woodview Farm – Overseal – Mount Pleasant Barn – Acresford – Donisthorpe – Short Heath

Distance: 3.75 miles (6km)

Start: Parking place at Short Heath, at the junction with the access to Woodview Farm. Grid reference: 304149

Map(s): OS 1:25000 Pathfinder Series No. 873, Ashby de la Zouch

How to get there:

By Public Transport: Monday to Saturday bus service from Ashby and Burton to Short Heath.

By Car: A444 to Overseal, then follow signs to Moira. Take the first right turn beyond Overseal. The parking place is 500 metres on the right, at the junction with the access track to Woodview Farm.

The Pub

The Cricketts Inn at Acresford is the most southerly pub in Derbyshire. A short jump out of the bar and you're in Leicestershire. There has been a pub on this site since at least 1753. Inevitably, in a place so old, there's supposed to be a resident ghost. Reputedly the ghost is that of a previous landlord. Perhaps he's still keeping an eye on the place, particularly the beer, for it is very good. Bass, Marstons and a guest beer are usually on offer. Food is served at lunchtimes and evenings daily. Opening hours are 11.00am – 3.00pm and 6.30pm –11.00pm Monday to Saturday, 12.00noon – 2.30pm and 7.00pm – 10.30pm on Sundays. A grand pub with a well deserved reputation. There is seating outside, but the A444 is uncomfortably close.

The Walk

From the road junction at Short Heath, follow the track signed to Woodview Farm. At the bungalow, there is a stile in the hedge on the right, taking you into fields. Go straight across the field, heading towards the gate in the far left-hand corner. Overseal is in view ahead. Just before you reach the gate in the corner, there is a stile in the left-hand fence. Go over this stile, and its nearby twin, to gain entry to another field. The map shows the path bearing right across this field, though there is no sign of it on the ground. The map then shows another path, running back along the far boundary of the field to a point opposite to that where you are standing.

It doesn't take an expert map reader to realise that, instead of going round two sides of a triangle, it would be possible to cut off the corner, by simply heading across the field alongside the left-hand fence. However, this would not be on the right of way, so bear right and go diagonally across the field until you reach the track at the far side, where you should turn left. The track may well be defended by an electric fence, but it is easily surmounted. Follow the track alongside the hedge, until you reach a gateway. The track continues through the gateway, but your route lies to the right, over a decrepit "stile", which is barely distinguishable from a fence.

An Unusual Crop

In this next field, bear left, heading for a gap in the fence to the right of the three trees. This takes you into a further field, with an interesting crop of old vehicles. There seems to be an idea abroad that old vehicles and farm machinery, like horses that have past their working life, can be put out to grass in the sure and certain hope that they will eventually die. Someone ought to explain that this does not really happen to metal objects and that the result is reminiscent of a scrapyard rather than a farm.

Head across the field towards the right of the house. Try to ignore the Alsatians, whose bark is worse than their bite – at least it is as long as the securing chain doesn't snap! Go through the gate on the right, near to the house, then through the double gates on the left, to reach the driveway. The house obviously postdates the OS map, but if you turn right, along the drive you will soon reach the main A444 road and there is a footpath sign confirming that the drive is indeed the right of way.

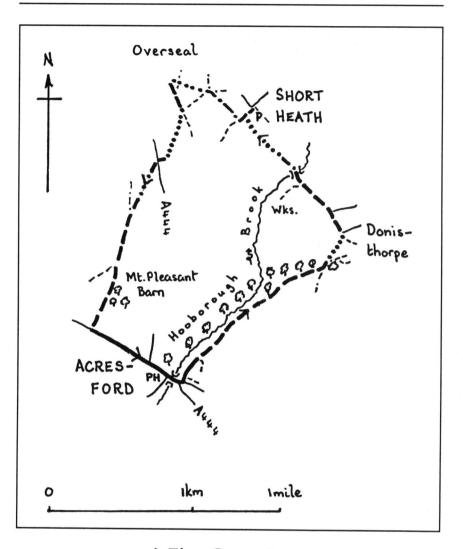

A Fine Green Lane

Cross the road and go through the gate opposite. Once in the field, do not go through the next gate on the right, but walk alongside the right-hand fence on what looks like the remains of an old road, an obvious flat area, now grassed over. Go through the next gate, by the electricity pole and continue alongside the fence, though it should now be on your left. The field narrows almost to a point. Here there is another gate and your suspicions about the old road are confirmed, for you now enter an overgrown green lane, which, if it was cleared, could easily have accommodated carts. Despite being shown on the map as a footpath, there is strong evidence that the lane is used by horses. Part way along the lane you will pass a footpath sign, pointing back the way you have just come. This oddity is explained by a glance at the map, which shows the green lane crossing a parish boundary at this point. South of the sign, in the parish of Netherseal, the route is an unclassified county road. North of the sign, in the parish of Overseal, it is a footpath. The law is that footpaths must be signed from the point where they leave the public road network, hence this fingerpost. The fact that the two bits of route are indistinguishable from one another is irrelevant.

Continue down the lane, noting for future reference the huge clump of blackberries on the left. Cadborough Farm is on the right with its driveway marked by a twin row of trees. However, before the driveway is reached, the lane bears right and here the footpath goes straight on, over a stile. The stile is waymarked and the path in the field ahead is well defined.

A Good View South

Head for the nearest corner of the wood, then follow the right-hand edge of the trees, to reach the ruins of Mount Pleasant Barn. There is an extensive view southwards from here, looking beyond Netherseal into Leicestershire, Staffordshire and Warwickshire. Prior to 1897 Netherseal was part of Leicestershire. Continue alongside the wood until you reach a gap in the hedge at the end of the field. The path continues straight on, running roughly parallel with the left-hand hedge, but 50 metres from it. You are heading towards two posts, seen ahead and to the right of the more distant clump of trees. The two posts turn out to be footpath signs on either side of the Coton to Acresford road. Descend to the road and turn left.

Walk along the road, taking great care, as there is no footway and in places the verge isn't up to much either. Fortunately, there is not too much traffic, but it does tend to come at higher speeds than you might find comfortable. Soon the junction with the A444 is reached and here at least there is a footway. Turn right and follow the main road down to the Cricketts Inn.

Into Leicestershire

On leaving the pub, cross the Netherseal to Acresford road and go over the bridge which spans the Hooborough Brook, thus leaving Derbyshire behind and entering Leicestershire. Cross the main road, which is very busy and fast, then bear left at the junction, up the Measham road. Just beyond the first buildings, go left, leaving the road and passing in front of the cottages. At the far end of the cottages, continue ahead until the track swings to the right. Here bear left to reach a waymarked gate. The broad track forks just after the gate. The more used arm goes right, but this only leads into an old quarry. Keep on the left-hand arm which continues at a lower level, just inside the wood. Paths leave and join at various points but none of them are official and at points where there is any likelihood of mistake there are waymarks. This is a curious area. The path runs alongside the wood which fringes the brook, but the path itself is often perched on an embankment, with what look like overgrown ponds on the right. Beyond the "ponds" can be seen the grassed-over remains of the quarry, with a variety of rock types visible. Eventually the path bears right and climbs up by the fence to emerge into open fields. This is at variance with the map, but the route is waymarked so it is suggested that you follow it. There are warning notices, threatening dire consequences for anyone entering the wood. Discretion being the better part of valour, the author did not investigate the truth of these.

Donisthorpe

Carry on by the top of the wood along the field path. Pass through a stile and continue alongside the wood, descending now towards Donisthorpe. The village and pub can be seen ahead on the hillside. The path now dips to reach a kissing gate at the end of the wood. A muddy patch follows and then you begin the ascent to Donisthorpe. Various paths are obvious in this field, but yours is the one which bears left, heading up to the left of the white house.

As you breast the rise there seems to be no way out in this corner of the field, but there is a gateway in the top left-hand corner, hidden by the blockwork building on the left. Here there is another kissing gate. Make sure you like your walking companions as tradition suggests you kiss the person who comes through behind you. Carry straight on, ignoring the turning to the right and passing the blue tanks on the left. A rough track runs along the fronts of the houses, with open fields to the left and a grand, extensive view. At the end of the houses, the track continues across the fields and Short Heath is in view ahead. On the right, as you enter the field, is a recumbent waymarker. Attempts to follow its directions would entail either excavations or flying.

Beware Rotten Planks

Follow the track down the field until you near the bottom. Here the track turns left, heading towards the water treatment works. The path drops off to the right, meandering across the muddy field to a metal bridge over the Hooborough Brook again. You are back in Derbyshire. The planks on the bridge leave a good deal to be desired. One at least is rotten.

Up the field you go, with the hedge on your right. Scramble over a stile and still head upwards, towards Woodview Farm, seen ahead. Another stile and then you realise that the bungalow which you saw at the beginning of the walk is built across the line of the path. Resisting the temptation to climb through the first window, go through the kitchen and out through the front door, bear right and avoid the bungalow and its garden altogether.

This field is another wonderful example of farm machinery being put out to grass. There is a stile of sorts in the hedge in the midst of the junk, but it may be easier to head for the gate in the right-hand corner of the field. This takes you out onto the road exactly at the starting point of the walk.

24: SNELSTON

The Route: Snelston Church – Snelston Village – Littlefields Lane –Toadhole Bridge – Church Mayfield – Dove Bridge – Clifton – Margery Bower –Mountpleasant Farm – Snelston Park – Snelston Church.

Distance: 4.4 miles (7km)

Start: Lay-by in front of Snelston Church, Grid reference: 155433

Map(s): OS 1:25000 Pathfinder Series No. 810, Ashbourne and Churnet Valley

How to get there:

By Public Transport: Monday to Saturday bus service to Clifton from Ashbourne.

By Car: A515 from Ashbourne or Sudbury, then follow the signs to Snelston.

The Pub

The Cock Inn at Clifton serves Bass beers. It is an old pub and used to be the focal point for a small market in agricultural produce. Now it is a friendly local, with opening hours 11.00am – 2.30pm and 7.00pm – 11.00pm, Monday to Friday, (closed on Monday lunchtimes), 11.00am – 3.00pm and 6.30pm – 11.00pm on Saturdays, with usual Sunday hours. Food is served at lunchtimes, Tuesdays to Sundays and in the evening, Thursday to Sunday. Families are welcomed and there is a garden area where you can sit and watch a round of golf while you quaff your ale.

The Walk

The walk starts from in front of St. Peter's church at Snelston. This was extensively rebuilt in the early part of this century, but it is an attractive church despite that and it contains a 13th century font. Walk down the road towards the village, going straight ahead at the junction by the telephone box, to reach the T-junction. The village is very attractive, with no two houses having the same window design, yet all looking as if they belong. The Harrison family who held the estate in the 19th century, commissioned the architect Cottingham to completely redesign the village. The fine building on the opposite side of the T-junction is the former Stanton Arms pub. Indeed, it is still shown as such on the latest Pathfinder map. As it had only a six-day licence it would not have been much good for your average Sunday walker. Snelston village used to have two pubs, but now has none. The other was the Three Horseshoes, which lay just to the left at the T-junction, down by the bridge.

One that got away: The former Stanton Arms

Snelston Popular Front

Turn right at the T-junction by the war memorial, noting with some amusement the seat donated by the Snelston Popular Front, a title more usually given to fanatical nationalist groups than village conservation societies. Perhaps there was once a Snelston Nationalist Movement and this is its sole legacy. Follow Littlefield Lane as it bends to the left and leaves the village behind. The lane is very narrow in parts, but fortunately sees little traffic. Soon you crest the slight rise out of the village and begin the descent towards the Dove.

At the T-junction where Littlefield Lane meets the main road, go straight ahead, through a signposted gate. A track heads straight across the field to the left of the hut, before descending an oddly out of place cutting. There is stile and gate in the cutting, which turns out to be the remains of a bridge under the former Uttoxeter to Ashbourne railway. The route of the railway itself is virtually indistinguishable from the surrounding fields now. Beyond the railway the track continues to a footbridge, known by the unattractive name of Toadhole Bridge. The name may refer to toads, but not uncommonly it is a corruption of the common expression "t'owd", meaning "the old". In which case, what was the "hole"? The bridge spans the River Dove and thus takes you into Staffordshire.

Snelston Church

Along the River Dove

Go straight on with the fence to your left, ignoring the stile on the left, and heading for the thorn bushes and the notice board. You soon come close to the river bank on your right. Keeping close company with the

Dove, pass through a couple of stiles and avoid falling in at the weir. Another stile soon follows, after which the path cuts off a loop of the river, heading instead for a clump of thorns in mid field and then for a gateway by the two beech trees.

In the next field, keep straight on, but beware, the path forks in mid field. Ignore the stile to the left and head for the gate way instead. If you find that you have a wall or boundary of any description, other than the flood banks, between you and the river, you are in the wrong field!

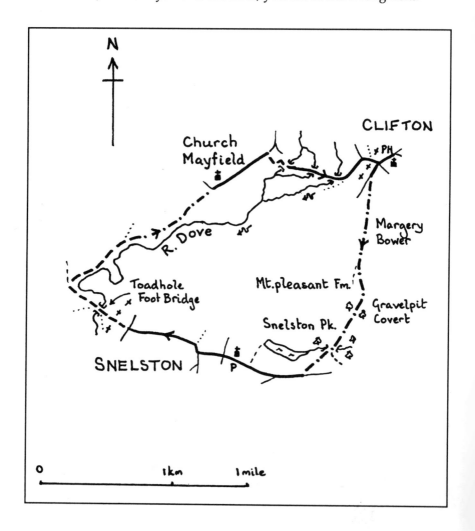

There is a temptation in this next field to follow the wall to the left, but this should be resisted and you should bear right instead, keeping company with the river. The tower of Church Mayfield Church is now in view ahead and is a useful guide. The next objective is the metal gate seen ahead. Once this has been negotiated, head for the church, ignoring the obvious track leading away to the left. Your path now runs close to the river bank, but the river is hidden by high flood banks and bushes. This could be a tricky walk after a lot of heavy rain. Soon another stile is reached, in the corner of the field nearest to the river. This takes you onto a small footbridge over a tributary stream and through another stile on the far side. Bear left in this next field, heading uphill towards the dead trees and in this manner reach a gap in the hedge in the top right-hand corner. Keep on the right in the next field to another gap in the hedge. The field you have just left, and the one you now enter, have a curiously manicured appearance, almost like a golf course. Still keep to the right, heading towards the church tower and so reach a stile in the corner of the field. Here you join the road.

Church Mayfield

Turn right, along the road, which appropriately is called Church Lane and soon pass the church of St. John Baptist on your left. Church Mayfield is a curious mixture of ancient and modern buildings. There are some very fine old properties. Soon a row of cottages is reached on the left-hand side. Almost at the end of the row, opposite Dove Cottage, go right along a tarred footpath which has a No Cycling sign. The path passes across the front of a group of white houses then, near the twin chimneys of the works, it does a quick left and right to descend to the bridge over the mill race. Once over the mill race go left, along the backs of the cottages. At the gap between the rows of cottages go right and so reach the road in front of the mill and the houses. The houses are stone and the whole place has the unmistakeable air of a South Pennine mill village, curiously out of place in this corner of Staffordshire. Follow the road alongside the river and soon cross the bridge over the Dove to re-enter Derbyshire.

From the Dove Bridge there is a fine view up the valley to the Peak District, with Thorpe Cloud being visible. The mill road continues its level course across the flood plain of the Dove, crossing the Henmore Brook before turning left alongside the former Ashbourne – Uttoxeter railway. It looks as if the road may at one time have been a railway siding, for there is a gate at a rather odd angle in the fence between the road and the railway, just near the bend. Continue on the road to its junction with Watery Lane and here go right. The former railway is crossed at once. Note the fine station buildings of Clifton station on the right, now in private ownership and in use as a house. The road now slopes steeply up through a rock cutting. There is neither footway nor verge in the cutting, but there seems to be marginally more room for safety on the left-hand side. Fortunately there is little traffic on this road and it is only a very short distance to the cross roads in Clifton village.

Public Transport Users Start Here

Public transport users will join the walk in Clifton, alas not now arriving by train but by the much less frequent buses.

At the cross roads, if you're heading for the pub, go left. The Cock Inn is just on the brow of the hill a few yards away opposite Holy Trinity Church. At one time the pub served as a focus for a small market, but this has long since ceased. The local branch of the Smith clan made a considerable fortune out of cheese and used some of the cash to endow Clifton church.

Imbibing finished, retrace your steps to the cross roads and go straight on to reach a footpath sign on the left-hand side of the road, at the end of the brick wall. Scramble through the hedge into the field and head diagonally across the field towards a large tree. It soon becomes clear that some of the field boundaries shown on the OS map have been removed and the route is by no means obvious underfoot. At the big ash tree there is the remnant of a hedge and you will find a stile by the holly bush, in what was once the field corner.

A Civil War Skirmish

The route in the next field is even less obvious, but you should continue straight ahead up the middle of the field on the crest of the ridge. Soon, the trees that surround Margery Bower can be seen ahead and these make an excellent guide. From any point on this ascent there is a superb view over the southern Peak District, with Thorpe Cloud and Minninglow clearly seen. However, you should be warned that when this walk was tested, there was a bull and a herd of cows in this field. They were well hidden by the slope of the land, but made a bee-line for us when we were spotted! The advice is not to stop to admire views until you reach the trees at Margery Bower. Escape is then a feasible proposition. The trees mark the site of a tumulus, but this place was also the spot where Parliamentary troops set up a gun battery to harry retreating

Royalist forces during the Civil War. A cannon ball from that affray is preserved in Ashbourne church.

Your line of advance from this point lies through the stile by the gate just to the right of the trees. This takes you onto a broad track, quite muddy in places and with a curious wide ditch alongside on the left. Just before the next gate is reached, bear left into this depression to pick up a sketchy path, running almost parallel with the track you have just left. Follow this path through an area of damp scrub to reach a gate – no stile. Scale the gate into the field and head across to the top left-hand corner.

Less Than Pleasant

Mount Pleasant Farm is on the right, but the name is most inappropriate when it comes to the passage of this particular field. It is a quagmire of the highest order, not helped by the incipient stream you have to cross half way. With your boots now weighing three times as much as they did before you started the traverse, climb up to reach the left-hand fence and follow this to a gate and stile in the corner, to the left of the tall trees. The final straw to this Somme like passage, was the presence of an electric fence a short way before the stile.

Snelston Park

Go over the stile and turn right, alongside the fence, heading now for Gravelpit Covert. At the wood there is a stile, which to your intense surprise turns out to be waymarked! The path descends easily and obviously through the wood to another waymarked stile at the far side. Do not attempt to climb this stile. There are much easier ways of negotiating it, but telling you how would spoil the fun. Here you enter the parkland which surrounded Snelston Hall. There is a grand view over the park from this point. Of particular interest are the lake and the nearby stand of monkey puzzle trees, said to be the first successfully grown in this country. These were planted by the Harrison family in the 19th century, when Snelston Hall and its park were completely remodelled. The hall was built in 1828 in Gothic revival style, but was demolished in 1951, having been empty for some years. The parkland extended to 300 acres and there were 30 acres of formal gardens as well. The present owners of the estate, the Stantons, live in the converted stable block, which is a fine building in its own right and certainly more functional than the hall it replaced.

Descend through the park to the gap between the wood of Lower Dumble and the trees fringing the lake. Here there is a stile by a gate. Ignore other stiles and gates going into the woods. Go through the gap and resist the temptation to bear left up the obvious track. Instead, bear right, heading uphill to the right of the solitary tree. There is no obvious path or way out of the park at this stage, but, as you round the end of the hill you will see a fence on your right and a line of trees and bushes on your left. Where these two converge is the point where you will find the gate and stile that take you out onto Windmill Lane. Snelston church and your car lie about 500 yards downhill to the right.

25: SPINKHILL

The Route: Spinkhill – Chesterfield Canal towpath – Renishaw –Norbriggs branch – Happy Valley – Grange Farm – Barlbro' – Barlbro' Hall –Parkhall Farm – Spinkhill

Distance: 7.9 miles (12.75km)

Start: Car park opposite the church. Grid reference: 454785

Map(s): OS 1:25000 Pathfinder Series No. 762, Worksop South and Staveley

How to get there:

By Public Transport: Daily service from Sheffield. Public transport users from Chesterfield or Staveley should use the Monday to Saturday service to Renishaw.

By Car: A616 from Sheffield or M1. Spinkhill is signed from this road.

The Pub

The Angel Hotel in College Road, Spinkhill, sells Tetleys, Marstons and Whitbread beers. There's also a regular guest beer. The landlord intends to develop the traditional cellar area for wine tasting events. What with the beers and the wine it is suggested that this is a pub best visited after the walk than before. After your session in the pub you'll be prepared to believe in the resident ghost! Opening hours are 12.00noon – 3.00pm and 7.00pm – 11.00pm on Monday to Friday, 11.00am – 11.00pm on Saturday, 12.00noon – 3.00pm and 7.00pm – 10.30pm on Sundays. Food is served lunchtimes and evenings daily.

The Walk

The start of the walk is the car park opposite the church. At first glance the church looks like any ordinary parish church anywhere in England, but it is unusual. The dedication gives the game away, for this is the Church of the Immaculate Conception. In other words, it is Roman

Catholic, closely connected to the nearby school or College of Mount St. Mary's. Spinkhill was a Roman Catholic enclave in a sea of Protestantism after the Reformation, largely due to the influence of the Pole family of Spinkhill Hall. The present college is built around the hall, which contains a private chapel that was never discovered throughout the religious persecution that followed the break with Rome. The chapel is still in use. The church, built in 1840, was designed by Hansom, who is more widely known for his design of the Hansom Cab.

The Church of The Immaculate Conception, Spinkhill

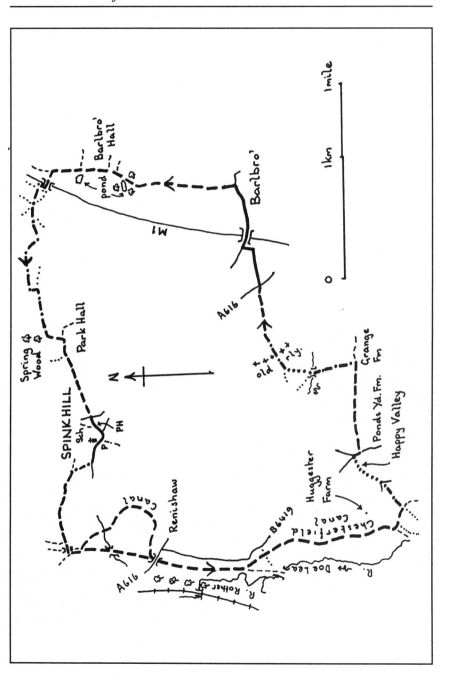

From the car park turn left and walk down the road for a short distance
until you reach a stile by a gate on the right. This takes you onto the
playing fields of the college. The path skirts to the right of the rugby
posts and to the right of a clump of trees, heading towards the corner of
the field, by the football goalposts. A track is soon joined and this is
followed to a gateway by six trees. After that you are out of danger from
sportsmen or from oddly shaped projectiles covered in leather. The view
from the gateway is quite extensive over towards the suburbs of Sheffield. The water tower at Norton is clearly seen. Follow the track gently
downhill into the Rother valley.

Reminders of the Canal and Railway Ages

Just beyond the pylon the track crosses a bridge. This spans the course of
the Chesterfield canal and the former Gt. Central Railway. Both are now
disused and along both there is now a public footpath. Short of jumping,
there is no access to either at this point, so cross the bridge and go left at
the T-junction at the far end. The track now descends to "rail" level. Of
particular note is the shallow cutting on the right-hand side just before
you reach the level of the railway. This marks the 18th century alignment of the canal. It was extensively rebuilt in the closing years of the
19th century in order to accommodate the new railway. The canal line
you crossed earlier is thus modern by canal standards and had a
working life of less than thirty years, closing in 1908.

Where the track forks, go left through a kissing gate, onto the old
railway. You have a choice here. You may either turn right, along the
railway, now one of Derbyshire County Council's Trails, or you can
cross the railway, go through the stile onto the towpath and then go
right, along the canal alignment. The railway is the shorter of the two,
but the canal is the more historic, (this being the original alignment). It
has to be said that the canal route passes uncomfortably close to an iron
works and the scenery is not of the best. There's no water in the cut
either, so unless you really are a canal enthusiast, the railway route is
preferable.

Renishaw has been the scene of iron and coal working since the middle
of the 17th century, when the Sitwell family of Renishaw Hall began the
exploitation of the local coal and ironstone measures. The industries
enjoyed a period of great prosperity during the 18th and 19th centuries,
but have now mainly vanished.

Welcome Restoration

The railway crosses over a high embankment, now well grown with trees. The canal has diverged at this point. A bridge takes the line over the Spinkhill road. A brisk walk on virtually flat ground soon brings you to the remains of Renishaw station and the canal rejoins from the left, just before the blue brick bridge. Go through one of the many gaps onto the towpath and continue along the canal. There are extensive restoration works going on here and a new sluice has been constructed. There is an ambitious project to restore this canal to navigation. Already a considerable section has been restored at the Chesterfield end, a vast improvement on the dereliction that existed only a few years earlier. Walkers on this route can expect to see further works as the restoration project advances.

Continue along the towpath, which now begins to draw away from the railway. Ignore paths deviating from the towpath and continue over the rough lane where the bridge has been demolished, into the fields on the far side. Here the canal has been virtually eliminated altogether. Only the towpath line and the remains of the right-hand boundary fence giving any clue as to its previous existence. Staveley church can be seen away to the right and the houses of Mastin Moor ahead. The corner of the field is soon reached and the towpath pursues its unerring course. There is even less evidence of the canal here as the whole field has been ploughed. Only a slightly different colour of soil on the left gives a clue. Soon the canal line can be seen ahead where it swings right to cross the shallow valley of the Doe Lea Brook. The embankment can be seen and the wide breach where the aqueduct once stood. This aqueduct was the subject of some dispute in the early days of the canal, when the other users of the waters in the Rother and Doe Lea sought to restrict the canal company's supply. The original proposal for the canal would have had no aqueduct at this point, but would have had a further two locks. The aqueduct saved the expenditure on the locks and retained the use of water which came into the canal from the Rother at the Chesterfield end.

Onto the Norbriggs Branch

At the gap in the hedge, the canal suddenly reappears on the left as a ditch, but not for long. Cross over the stile and skirt to the right of Huggester Farm, still on the towpath line. Now the canal appears properly as a broad overgrown embankment with a dry ditch in the top. The path now forks. Go left, heading towards the houses of Mastin Moor. This section of canal is virtually intact, though very overgrown.

You have now left the main line and are forging ahead along the Norbriggs branch canal. In a short while you go left, over a footbridge and leave the canal behind.

Happy Valley

A sketchy path leads up alongside the right-hand hedge of the field, to the point where the hedge does a pronounced right-hand kink. Here you bear left across the field, heading to the left of the barn and keeping company with the remains of a fence. There is a gateway in the far left-hand corner of the field and this lands you on the driveway to Happy Valley Farm. Cross the track and go straight on, keeping Happy Valley on the left, and thus reach a stile in the hedge ahead. Carry straight on in the next field, heading for the electricity pole. There is a stile in the left-hand corner of the field. In the next field the path makes a bee-line for the stile to the right of the signpost and so you reach the B6419 road. Spinkhill church spire can be seen to the left.

At the road, go right for about 100 metres and then at the brow of the hill, go left, along a classic green lane, hedged on either side. As you climb the gentle hill, it is worth stopping every now and then to gaze back over the Doe Lea and Rother valleys, for the view is very extensive, reaching right over to the Peak District moors. When you reach Grange Farm, leave the track and go left and descend the field alongside the left-hand hedge, ignoring a more obvious track which tends to the right, across the field.

By Devious Means to Barlbro'

At the bottom of the field, in the left-hand corner, there is a well-hidden plank bridge and stepping stones across the brook and its accompanying marshy area. The map now suggests that the path should bear away to the left in the next field, heading towards Beightonfields Priory, which is not visible at this point. A marker on this route is the electricity pole in mid field. Beyond this, when you come level with the buildings of Beightonfields on your left, you should turn sharp right and head across the field to reach a gap in the hedge in the top corner. Why doesn't he mention the various field boundaries shown on the map, you may wonder? For the simple reason that most have been grubbed up and there is nothing to navigate by at all. It does seem that other users of this route pay scant regard to the niceties of rights of way and, on crossing the bridge mentioned earlier, they bear right and follow the right-hand hedge up to the top of the field and the gap.

Go through the gap and then straight across the next field, in which there is no obvious path. You should head for the right-hand end of the embankment, just where it merges with the field. Cross the erstwhile railway line, which once ran from Sheffield to Langwith, and continue on a good path alongside the right-hand hedge of the field. The path soon assumes the proportions of a track and then becomes concreted. Go along this track, passing the former colliery site on the left, now completely overgrown, and so reach the A616. This is a busy dual carriageway linking south Sheffield to the M1, so take care when crossing.

Barlbro' Village

Go across the main road and straight on along the lane marked with the 3T sign. You pass a number of houses on the left, but your line of march is brought to an abrupt halt by the cutting containing the M1. Discretion being the better part of valour, you would do well to turn left at this point, go down Westfield Lane to the T-junction and turn right at that point to cross the M1 on the bridge provided. In this manner you enter Barlborough. This is an ancient village, though you have to look hard to see evidence of it among the new brick houses. Every now and then there are buildings made in the characteristic limestone of this area, for Barlbro' sits on the same limestone ridge as Bolsover and Hardwick. Manor Cottage, on the right-hand side as you walk up the main street, is built in this mellow stone. There is no dearth of pubs in this village and you pass the Royal Oak, (Stones) and the Apollo, (Wards), before turning left just opposite the post office. Follow the road, with the school on the right, until you reach a track going straight ahead as the road goes left. The track runs along the backs of houses for a short way before emerging from the village. There is an extensive view to the left, over Spinkhill to Sheffield and beyond to the high land near Penistone. On the right is the local playing field, but when you have walked beyond this, you are alongside the boundary of Barlbro' Hall. You will catch occasional glimpses of the hall through the trees on the right, but it is a very secretive place.

Barlbro' Hall and Park

A track leads away to the left, but your route still lies alongside the Barlbro' Hall boundary. Barlbro' Hall was designed by the noted Elizabethan architect Smythson in 1583, for the de Rhodes family. One noted member of this clan was one of the judges at the trial of Mary, Queen of Scots. The track dips into a small wood, with a pond on the left. There are some ancient buildings on the right, now in a sad state of repair, with blocked windows. Just beyond the wood, the track forks three ways. Barlbro' Hall lies to the right, but closer inspection is not encouraged. Indeed the notices are decidedly unfriendly. Your path lies straight ahead and you will get your best view of the hall from this point. The ghost of a grey lady is supposed to haunt the hall. She is reputedly the daughter of one of the previous owners and her fiance was killed en route to their wedding.

A short distance further on, the track goes right, but there is a stile in the fence ahead, alongside the double gates.

The broad path continues through Barlbro' Park, another example of the classic English "informal" park, with tree clumps strategically placed to enhance the view from the big house.

The path passes a pond on the left and the footbridge over the M1 can be seen ahead. This is your next objective, but it is worth looking back to the hall from this point, to see how well it blends into the artificial landscape created round it. As you come level with the footbridge, go left, leaving the track and going through the kissing gate. Cross the M1 and at the far side of the bridge go right to reach another kissing gate.

Where Footpaths Move

This gate is waymarked left and right. You go left. The sharp eyed among you will now notice that the route described bears little resemblance to that shown on the current edition of the Pathfinder map. Nevertheless, the route in this book is the waymarked path and the rights of way shown on the OS map do not exist on the ground. The fences in this area all seem to be of a uniform age and it looks as if the opportunity was taken to rationalise the footpath system at the same time. You are advised to follow the book. Follow the left-hand fence to reach a stile in the corner of the field. The stile is conspicuously waymarked straight on and right. Go straight on, still with the fence to your left to reach a brace of waymarked stiles. Negotiate them both and again go straight on, but now the fence is to your right, along with a new plantation.

At the corner of the plantation, the map shows a dotted line, not a right of way, heading across the field. However, there is a waymark here which directs you right, alongside the boundary fence. Follow the waymarks round the field and thus complete three sides of a rectangle. As you follow the final leg of the trip round the field there is a good view over towards Spinkhill, with the church spire being obvious and a pleasant view back towards Barlbro' Hall. Look out for a waymarked stile on the right and having found it, go over it, leaving the deviations behind.

Return to Spinkhill

Go straight on now, with the fence to your right, along a good track. Park Hall Farm is in view ahead and the dome of Mount St. Mary's College. The dome was designed by Gilbert Scott in the 1920s. Follow the track through the gateway and then bear left, still following the track as it heads towards the farm. As you reach the buildings, keep straight on. Do not turn right into the farm yard, but wait until you have past the farm then go right, along the lane. On your left is Park Hall, a fine Elizabethan building, now serving as a hotel. Follow the lane, which is soon joined by the driveway from the hotel. At the cross roads at the end of the lane, go straight ahead into Spinkhill village. The Angel is on your left and if you came by car, the car park lies a little further on, through the village, round the right-hand bend, opposite the church.

26: STAINSBY

The Route: Stainsby Mill – Blingsby Gate – Hardwick Hall – Hardwick Inn – Hardstoft – Astwith – Stainsby

Distance: 5.4 miles (8.75km)

Start: Car park near Stainsby Mill, Grid reference: 456654

Map(s): OS 1:25000 Pathfinder Series No. 779, Mansfield North and part of Sherwood Forest

How to get there:

By Public Transport: There is no public transport to Hardwick or Stainsby, but there is a daily service between Chesterfield and Nottingham which calls at Hardstoft, part way round the walk. Alight at the Shoulder of Mutton.

By Car: From the M1/A617 junction at Heath, follow the signs for Hardwick Hall. The route takes you back under the M1 and soon reaches Stainsby Mill. You should park at this point.

The Pub

The Hardwick Inn, near Hardwick Hall, enjoys a well-deserved reputation for good ale and food. It is not in a village, but is sited at the exit gate from Hardwick Park. It is a fine stone built pub with a large and pleasant beer garden to the rear. The landlord has published his own book on the history of the pub from 1607. Opening hours are 11.30am – 3.00pm and 6.30pm – 11.00pm Monday to Saturday, 12.00noon – 3.00pm and 7.00pm –10.30pm on Sundays. Food is served daily except Sunday evenings, in the bars and the restaurant. The menu is mouth watering. The beers on offer are Youngers and Theakstons.

The Walk

Stainsby Mill is a National Trust property and is well worth a visit. However, you are advised to make the visit after you have done the walk. Check the opening times before you set off. Walk along the road past the mill and over the mill stream, noting the holding pond on the right. At the triangular junction bear right, still following the signs to Hardwick Hall. Soon you reach the pay booth, but pedestrians don't have to pay, only car users. Beyond the booth you enter Hardwick Park. Continue along the driveway in very pleasant surroundings, except for the ever present rumble of the nearby M1.

Stainsby Mill

Into Hardwick Park

This part of the park is cultivated, but soon the Blingsby Gate cattle-grid is reached and after that you are in real parkland. Beyond the second cattle-grid, the road bends to the left. Go straight on here alongside the fence and then make your way across to the stile in the fence surrounding the Row Ponds. Here you have a choice; either to go straight on through the next stile and directly up to the Hall, or to turn left and walk up past the ponds, steadily climbing until a stile is reached close to the main access road to the Hall. Either route is obvious underfoot and the Hall is the most impressive waymarker.

At the Hall you are strongly recommended to visit the gardens. (You are strongly recommended to visit the house as well, but not when you are

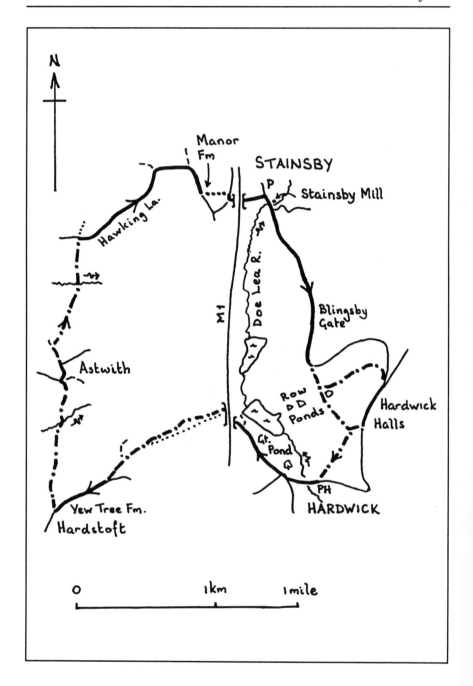

doing this walk). The "new" Hall was built at the command of the famous Bess of Hardwick. Her family initials ES, standing for Elisabeth Shrewsbury, adorn the frontage of the house and the garden walls. The remains of the older hall lie just in front of the new hall and these are now in the care of English Heritage. Bess of Hardwick is one of Derbyshire's great characters. She was born in 1518 and died in 1608, having had four husbands. In 1549, she bought the Chatsworth estate and built a mansion, which has since been replaced by the present house. She built the two halls at Hardwick, but it is recalled that her final husband, the Earl of Shrewsbury, who was reputedly the richest man in the kingdom when they married, died so poor that he could not even afford an executor!

On leaving the main entrance to the New Hall, go across the road and bear left, following the wall down, below the ruins of the old hall to reach the parkland again. The Hardwick Inn can be seen ahead and although there are official rights of way across the park, they are not obvious, because there is the freedom to wander at will. Make your way down to the gate beside the cattle-grid, close to the pub.

Hardwick Inn and the Great Pond

On leaving the pub, go left, bearing right at the junction with Stainsby Lane. At the next junction, keep right, walking alongside the boundary fence to Hardwick Park. Soon you will see Hardwick Great Pond on the right. This is supplied by the Row Ponds which you passed earlier. It is the favourite haunt of fishermen. Just beyond the pedestrian entrance to the Park, the road dives under the M1. At least under the bridge the noise is much reduced.

Beyond the M1, cross the road and go up the path on the left, by the fence. There is a stile on the left at the top of the cutting. This should be the start of your route through the fields according to the map. However, when the walk was investigated, no trace could be found of an exit stile at the far end of the field. The hedge was impassable to anyone other than a machete armed masochist. The author finally ignored the stile at the top of the cutting and carried on up the field, with the fence to the left. Skirt round to the right of the clump of trees at the top of the field to reach a gateway. There is a good view back to the Hall from this point. There is a view down the valley to Bolsover castle as well. Go through the gateway and then left to reach another gateway. Go through this as well and then turn right alongside the hedge. At this point you have rejoined the right of way as shown on the map.

Follow the hedge up on the right to reach a track, which joins from the right. Carry on still further, again with the fence on your right, to reach a stile by a gate. From this point, the various ponds in Hardwick Park can be seen. The path now tops the rise and begins to descend slightly. Keep the fence cum hedge on your right. Hardstoft is now in view ahead.

Who, Or What, Is "Konstsmide"?

Ignoring the gateway on the right, carry straight on to reach a stile by a further gate. This takes you out onto Deep Lane. Straight on again, up the lane to Hardstoft. You may like to try and get your tongue round the company name displayed on the buildings on the right. KONSTSMIDE is the name, but who they are or what they do is not stated. Opposite Yew Tree Farm and just beyond Konstsmide, go right, along a track and follow this down past Ash Lea Farm.

Go through the stile and into the fields, following the right-hand hedge until you reach the step stile. Having scrambled over this, continue alongside the same hedge, though now of course it is on your left. At the bottom of the field, there is a waymarked stile in the hedge. The path then heads across the next field to a gap in the hedge and dips to cross the stream. Astwith can now be seen ahead and the path is now more of a track and easily followed. It passes through a waymarked stile, by a gate to enter a rough lane. There is a view to the right to Hardwick Hall.

Astwith

Ignoring turnings to the left and right, you soon enter Astwith. Turn right, along the lane, at the waymark beyond the telephone box. The lane bends first to the left, then to the right. At the latter point, go straight on, along a waymarked track. Continue on this track until you reach a gate, just before the farm.

Go right here, over a waymarked stile and enter fields again. Bear left across the field to reach a stile by a gate, to the right of the ash tree. Continue down the next field, keeping the hedge to your left. Cross the stream in the bottom of the field to reach the stile alongside the gate. Beyond the stile, head up the left-hand side of the next field. Hardwick Hall is in view on your right. At the top of the field there is a stile in the left-hand corner. The path continues straight ahead, making for the left of the largest tree. Unfortunately the farmer has dumped some rather noxious cow muck across the line of the path. Unless you are a complete masochist you will skirt round to the right of this and resume the line of march beyond the obstruction. A gap in the hedge leads out onto Hawking Lane.

The map shows a series of field paths making their way to Stainsby on the northern side of Hawking Lane. However, closer acquaintance shows that these are difficult to trace. Thus the advice is to turn right, along the lane and come into Stainsby that way instead.

Stainsby Village and the return to Stainsby Mill

The map shows the site of an old chapel just before you reach Stainsby, but there's no sign of it on the ground. Follow the road, as it swings right and enters the hamlet of Stainsby. This is an attractive little spot, with some fine old buildings. At the tree in the middle of the road, go right and descend, passing the entrance to Manor Farm on the left. Where the road bends to the left, just by the speed limit sign, there is a footpath sign on the left. A scramble up from the road leads to a stile and thus into fields again. The all pervading sound of the M1 is now very clear. Go across the field, keeping parallel with the barn on the left. There is a stile in the hedge cum fence ahead, marked by a post. This takes you into the tree screen, which was designed to block the view of and noise from the M1.

The path winds down the cutting side onto the realigned Mill Lane, almost opposite the M1 bridge. Cross Mill Lane and go under the bridge, following the signs to Hardwick and Stainsby Mill. In a little over 200 metres you reach the war memorial on the left and arrive back at Stainsby Mill.

27: STANTON BY BRIDGE

The Route: Stanton by Bridge – The Hills – Woodend Cottage – Ingleby Toft – Seven Spouts Farm – Hangman's Stone – Foremark – Anchor Church –Ingleby – Manor Farm – Stanton by Bridge

Distance: 7.1 miles (11.5km)

Start: Roadside parking just off the A514 at Stanton. Grid reference: 373273

Map(s): OS 1:25000 Pathfinder Series No. 852, Burton on Trent

How to get there:

By Public Transport: Monday to Saturday bus service between Derby and Swadlincote. No bus service to Ingleby.

By Car: Follow the A514 from Derby or Swadlincote to Stanton by Bridge and then take the Ingleby road. Park just after you leave the A514.

The Pub

The John Thompson at Ingleby is a unique pub for Derbyshire and one of a tiny handful nationwide, for this pub brews its own beer. Grand stuff it is too. This fine whitewashed pub, close to the Trent, started brewing its own beer in 1977. For the less adventurous, there's also Marstons Pedigree. Hot food is served Tuesday to Saturday at lunchtimes, with sandwiches only on Sundays. Opening hours are 10.30am – 2.30pm and 7pm – 11pm Monday to Saturday, 12noon – 2.30pm and 7pm – 10.30pm on Sundays. There is a large beer garden with good views across to the river.

The Walk

From your parking spot, walk back towards the triangular junction in the centre of Stanton. Just before the A514 is reached, there is a footpath sign by the derestriction plates. Go right here, along a narrow footpath by the side of a house. On the left is a relatively new larch lap fence. The

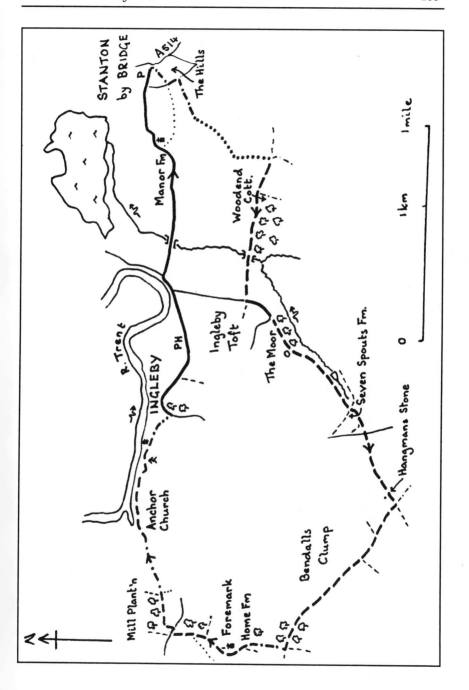

path emerges into a tumbled area of hummocks and hollows, trees and shrubs. On the right a path climbs to reach a prominent tree, by the farm machinery. This is not the way however, for your route lies to the left of the tall tree, down into the cutting. This is the area shown on the map as The Hills. Paths run hither and thither in all directions, but the main path is fortunately the one you want. It stays down in the cutting, keeping right at the most obvious fork, passing to the left of the farm machinery which is perched up on top of one of the hummocks. Soon a stile is reached and you will emerge out onto the back lane. Here go left and follow the lane until you reach the house named, Behind the Hills. Just beyond the house there is a white gate on the right. Go through this gate into the field with the farm machinery put out to grass. A fairly obvious track goes along the front of the derelict machines, but your route lies to the right, to a gateway in the fence.

In the next field, which shows evidence of ridge and furrow farming, go straight ahead, keeping about 30 metres from the left-hand hedge, with a pylon as a marker ahead. A gateway at the head of the field leads into another field which is very narrow. It may have been an old drove road rather than a field at one time. At the far end of this field there is a gateway, with no accompanying stile, nor an obvious means of opening the gate. Scramble over, preferably using the hinge end.

The next field displays no clear signs of a path, but the map shows that you should proceed diagonally left, keeping to the right of the pylon until you reach a stile and a bridge just a little way from the far left-hand corner. Follow the stream and the left-hand hedge until another bridge is reached in the far corner of this next field. The map indicates a bridleway joins at this point, but beyond the bridge there is no sign of it.

A Non-Existent Bridleway

Head straight across the field, though there's no obvious path. There is a line of wooden poles across the top of the field. Two of them have "lean to" supports. Head towards the right-hand one of these, keeping it somewhat to your left. Heavy going when the field has just been ploughed. When you reach the line of poles you also reach a good track. Here go right, by the side of a decrepit hedge. This is not shown on the map as a right of way, because, despite appearances it is actually a road! Carry on along the "road", passing Woodend Cottage on the left and ignoring the footpath sign pointing left. The "road" now deteriorates into a farm track as it passes through a gateway. To the right are good views over Ingleby to the Trent valley, while to the left lies West Wood.

The track descends gently alongside the wood which consists of a mixture of conifer plantation and hazel coppice. At the bottom of the hill the track crosses a culverted stream, there being extensive marshes left and right, with alders and willow scrub, a veritable haven for birdlife.

Fine Views across the Vale of Trent

Now the track rises away from the stream towards Ingleby Toft, which is the big house seen ahead. Again, as the track rises there is a view to the right over the Trent to Derby and the distant hills of the Peak District. Keep the hedge to your right and ascend to meet the narrow road, just opposite the entrance to Ingleby Toft. Here there is a signpost, pointing back the way you have just come, informing you that the route you've just been on is a bridleway. Nice to know you were acting within your rights, even in retrospect.

Turn left at the road and follow the lane until it turns sharply to the right. A track continues straight ahead through a gateway, with a wood on the left and what the map calls The Moor, on the right. The track dips to a very swampy, muddy area at the next gateway. The map shows a pond at this location, but it's not there now. Avoid the mud as best you can, and continue along the track, still with the wood on the left.

Seven Spouts and The Hangman's Stone

At the crossing of paths go straight on along the obvious track, now beginning the steady pull up towards Seven Spouts Farm. You pass a delightful little dam on the left and all the while there is the noise of the stream. Soon Seven Spouts Farm is reached. This has been impressively rebuilt with a glass fronted area overlooking the woodland. The map indicates that the Seven Spouts, from which the farm derives its name, lie down the track to the left. There has been extensive planting done here and there are a number of modern manholes in the bank-side on the right. Investigation revealed that there was only one spring now spouting from the hillside, so it's not really worth the deviation to find it.

At the farm the track splits. The route to the left went to the Seven Spouts as described above. The route to the right goes through Heath Woods to Foremark, but your route carries straight on, passing the glass fronted building before ascending to join the Ingleby – Ticknall road. A new access to the farm goes off to the right just before the road is reached, but you carry straight on, through a gateway and cross over the road. On the far side of the road continue through the fields, keeping close to the hedge on your left. A number of field boundaries have gone here, but the vital one, that on your left, is still extant. Keep a sharp look-out for a block of stone on your left. It is only a couple of feet high and set back into the hedge. This is shown on the map as the Hangman's Stone. A macabre name. Just beyond the stone the path dips to a gateway, beyond which there is a crossing of tracks. You go right here, alongside the hedge.

A track soon joins from the right but the bridleway carries straight on alongside the fence. Ignore the white sign pointing left and carry on along the broad track, past the stag headed oak tree. There is a wood on the right which does not appear on the map. Shortly afterwards the track enters the "new" wood at a gateway. Descend through the wood to reach a gate and stile at the bottom. This is the crossing of paths shown on the map just south of Home Farm.

Foremark, a church, a school and a farm

At the gate and stile at the end of the wood, go right and descend the shallow valley towards Home Farm. As you near the farm you will see two gates facing you. The lower one to the right is your route. It has an accompanying stile for good measure. Beyond the gate, the route runs between the older buildings of the farm, then bears left and ascends through another gateway. A further track joins from the left, then a big barn is passed, also on the left. (The route through the farmyard is waymarked in this direction, so you should have no trouble). Carry on along the track which soon swings to the right to skirt Foremark church. Approaching from this direction, the church is hidden until the last minute by a screen of yew trees. It has the unusual dedication of St. Saviour's.

As you come alongside the church there is a grand view over the Trent valley. The power station at Willington is particularly prominent, but it's far enough a way to simply be a feature in the landscape. One has to admit that the cooling towers do have a certain massive grace about them and can look quite attractive when the sun catches them. Continue down the track, ignoring the driveway going off to the right, which is the heavy lorry route into Repton Prep. School. Just beyond the driveway you will see the former Foremark Hall to the right. This is now part of the school. Continue down the track to the road and here go right for a short distance, before turning left at the next gateway.

The map suggests that the path should diverge left a little further along the road, but there is no sign of it in practice. Nor is there any sign of the direct route across the field as shown on the map. Instead, the path hugs the left-hand edge of the field down to the corner, then turns right, following the boundary of Mill Plantation. The path dips to a gateway beyond which an obvious track bears left. Your route lies straight on along the base of the slope. Eventually, as the crags are reached a good path develops. At the gap in the crags, the path continues straight ahead, over a fence in which there is no obvious stile.

Anchor Church, a refuge on a wet day

The route is then tightly constrained by the crags on the right and the old course of the Trent on the left. Soon the curious rock formation known as Anchor Church is reached. In part this is natural, a reminder of the power of the river to erode away the rocks, but there has been considerable human enlargement and addition to the natural caves. There are signs of very recent occupation and what looks like attempts to brick up some of the entrances. A fascinating place and very unusual in this otherwise gently rolling countryside. The path is right at river level here, so there could be problems in very wet weather. The pool in front of the "church" is known as the Black Pool, but any similarity with the Fylde coast resort ends with the name.

The name Anchor Church has been known for at least 300 years, but a 12th century legend tells of a treacherous priest who was bribed into beguiling a knight to leave his lady and his lands to go on crusade. On his return the knight found his place had been taken by another and suspecting his wife of duplicity killed her and the interloper. Stricken by remorse the priest confessed that the lady had been innocent and had been told her husband was dead. The knight spent his remaining days as a monk and the priest became a hermit at Anchor Church.

Eventually, just beyond Anchor Church you come alongside the Trent itself. Ignore the bridge on the left and carry on along the river bank until you reach a fence in which there is a gate and stile. Bear right here, away from the river and at the next fence, swing left, climbing up towards the pines. There is a grand view across the Vale of Trent from here and the village of Ingleby is in view ahead. Continue ahead, taking care not to get too close to the edge of the slope. You will spot an island in the river ahead and a stile on the bank to the right. This is tempting, but wrong. Your path stays higher up, following the fence on the right. Where a track veers off to the right, go straight on through a stile in the fence ahead, making a bee-line for Ingleby. The path bears right and descends to a gate in the wall. After that, keep the wall cum fence on your left and descend to the white gate. This takes you out onto the road and here you turn left.

Ingleby

Follow the road, which has an intermittent footway on the left-hand side. The lane swings right through the village of Ingleby, passing Yew Tree Cottage on the left and the bridleway sign on the right. There is a small pond on the right and then the war memorial and the tiny village hall. At the bend in the road, the footway finishes, just when you need it most. Take care at the bend. The pub is just a few metres ahead, so it would be a great shame to be a road casualty at this stage. The village name is Danish and on the hillside above the settlement there is a pagan Danish cemetery in Heath Wood.

On leaving the pub, turn left along the road again. There is a reasonable verge at this pint so it is quite safe. At the first road junction you are back alongside the Trent again, but you leave it at the next junction by turning right along the little lane signed to Stanton. The way ahead is clearly seen and it is ominously uphill. Cross the bridge and look right. You will see Woodend Cottage which you passed on your outward trek. Beyond the bridge the lane begins to climb gently away from the Trent. Where the road levels out, there is a view left over the valley. Particularly prominent is the lake, left behind after gravel extraction had finished. Quite an attractive feature now. Swarkestone Bridge can also be seen and after a few pints at the John Thompson one could be forgiven if one caught a glimpse of an army of Highlanders and heard the skirl of the pipes, for this was Bonnie Prince Charlie's furthest south. Swarkestone Bridge is basically 13th century. Legend has it that the bridge was built at the behest of two sisters whose lovers tragically drowned while trying to ford the Trent at that point.

Return to Stanton

The village of Stanton by Bridge soon comes into view and you reach Manor Farm on the left. The church of St. Michael's can be seen ahead, perched on top of the knoll. This is soon reached and it is worth a look, for it contains some Saxon and Norman workmanship, though it has been much rebuilt. The road continues, passing a well on the right and Brook House on the left. There is a slight dip as the culverted brook itself is crossed, then up you go, ignoring turnings to the right or left and thus you arrive back at the triangle from where you started.

28: TICKNALL

The Route: Ticknall – Middle Lodge – Standley's Barn – Calke Abbey –Calke Church – Staunton Harold Reservoir – White Leys Farm – Ticknall

Distance: 5.3 miles (8.5km)

Start: Public Car park off Ingleby Lane, Ticknall. Grid Reference: 352240

Map(s): OS 1:25000 Pathfinder Series No. 852, Burton on Trent

How to get there:

By Public Transport: Monday to Saturday service from Derby and Swadlincote. Seasonal Sunday service.

By Car: A514 from Derby or Swadlincote. The car park is signed in the village.

The Pub

The Wheel at Ticknall is a grand local pub, with two bars and real fires to welcome you on a cold winter's day. There is also a beer garden if it's really sunny. Home cooked bar snacks are served seven days a week. Children and ramblers are welcome and the ale is a lovely drop of Worthington or Bass on hand pump. The pub was built in the mid 18th century. The now disused top floor function room was apparently used at one time for local council meetings, a highly dubious practice. Several local residents were banished from the village for misdemeanours, probably related to the quantity of ale consumed at the council meetings. Hours of opening are "flexible" but Monday to Friday you should be sure of finding the door ajar from 12.00noon – 3.00pm and 7.00pm – 11.00pm. Similarly on Saturday between 11.30am and 11pm or on Sunday 12.00noon – 3.00pm and 7.00pm –10.30pm.

The Walk

From the car park, walk down to the main road. Here is the first major test of decision making, to go into the pub now or when you get back. The classic British compromise would be to go in now AND when you get back. Either way, spare some time to look round Ticknall itself. It is a picture postcard village, with beautiful front gardens, wayside water pumps and delightfully informal positioning of buildings. The old Ticknall church was pulled down in 1831 and a new one erected. Some remnants of the earlier church still survive. The village lock up, used until the First World War, also still survives, alongside the main road. The village owes much of its charm to its long association with the owners of Calke Abbey, the Harpur Crewe family. An eccentric bunch, the Harpur Crewes, refusing to allow motor vehicles into the park and closing rooms in the Abbey when they tired of them. The death of Charles Harpur Crewe in 1981 saw the estate pass to the National Trust in lieu of death duties.

Into Calke Park

On leaving the pub, go right, bearing right again at the antiques sign and footpath sign. Pass the tea rooms, the Coach House and the Malt House, noting the pump on the left. At the gate and stile by Bantons Cottage, you enter fields. Here bear right to join a path running alongside the wood on the far side of the field. This is Lodge Plantation and it forms a screen to Calke Park. At the gateway the path becomes a green lane and soon passes over the tunnel which carried the erstwhile Ticknall Tramway under the driveway. If you look to the right you will see the tunnel mouth. The tramway was not the sort you see in Blackpool or at Crich, but was an 18th century creation, horse worked, for carrying limestone from the nearby quarries, down to the Ashby Canal. The horses worked through the tunnel, but they must have walked with bent legs for the tunnel is not very high. At various points there are air and light grills in the roof, but you are strongly advised not to attempt the passage yourself.

The "Good Man" And His Fighting Cocks

Continue on the green lane, with the hedge on the right, passing the small pond on the left. Continue alongside the hedge, ignoring the stile. The broad green path has obviously been an old road at one time. There is soon another stile on the right and this too is passed by. Now the

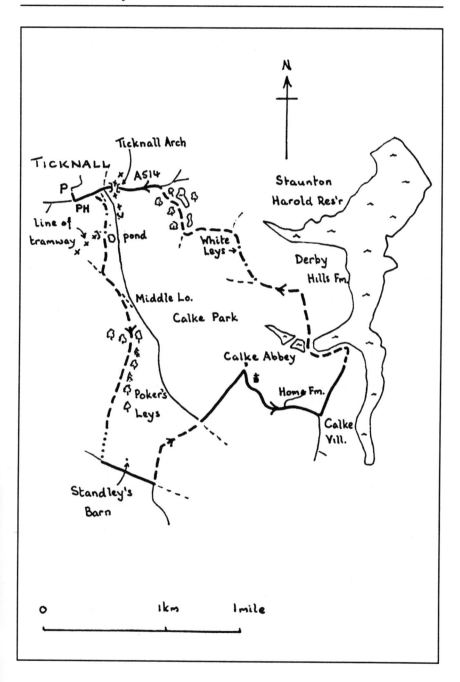

"road" swings away from the hedge, making its way towards the lodge gates, seen ahead. The main driveway to Calke Abbey is now very close on the left. The author remembers visiting the Abbey many years ago when the lodge was inhabited by the estate gamekeeper. He rejoiced in the wonderful name of Agathos Pegg. The name is Greek, meaning "the good man". He was a wonderful character, walking the bounds of the Park every morning, despite being well in his eighties, and keeping fighting cocks in his spare time!

Do not go through the lodge gates, but instead go over the stile by the third gate to the right of the lodge. This takes you out of the parkland and back into fields. Follow the track alongside the woodland on the left. A gateway leads the track into a narrow area of woodland. A further gate leads you out on the far side and you resume your course alongside the park fence on the left, with the fields on the right. There are many animal tracks emerging from the parkland. Some are obviously deer. All are considerably more agile than your average human as they have to negotiate a ditch, hedge and fence in a very short distance.

Standley's Barn

Continue along the track, which soon passes through another gateway over a culverted stream. The hedge and fence are still to your left until you reach the next gate and stile. Here the woodland ends and you stand in the corner of a large field. A track leads left, alongside the hedge, heading for Standley's Barn, seen to the left. However, this is not the footpath, nor is it a right of way. The path you want, heads for the third tree from the left, in the middle of the field. There is no obvious trodden route and the ground is deceptively soggy. There is evidence of ridge and furrow farming here, but the ridges are only marginally drier than the furrows. Beyond the trees, which are the remnants of a hedge, make for a stile which is marked by two tall posts. Thus you will end up on the lane, just to the right of Standley's Barn. Turn left here and proceed along the lane, ignoring the footpath sign to the right, until you come to the sharp right-hand bend. Here you leave the road and go left, (not straight ahead), through the gate or over the stile and so back into fields.

Keep the hedge on your right and follow the obvious track to a further gate, which doubles as a sheep pen and has a number of potential exits. The one you need has a stile, which would be an unusual means of exit for a sheep. Continue along the track, with the fence to your right, heading for the white gate. The higher land seen to the right here is Charnwood Forest.

Calke Abbey and Church

At the white gate you re-enter Calke Park and join the main driveway to the house. This is classic eighteenth century parkland, with its scattered trees. It is a delight to walk in, despite the cars. There is ample opportunity to escape from the road if you need to. Soon, on cresting a slight rise, Calke Abbey comes into view. It bears no resemblance at all to your concept of an Abbey, being a fine country house, the second largest in Derbyshire. Once the ancestral home of the Harpur-Crewe family, being built in 1703 for Sir John Harpur, it is now in the ownership of the National Trust and is open to the public. It is well worth a visit, though admission is by timed ticket as it is so popular. Even if you don't visit the house on this walk, make a resolution to do so on a future occasion.

At the junction just before the house, go right and follow the lane round the perimeter "ha ha" and up to the church. The map shows a right of way passing through the grounds of the mansion but this does not exist on the ground. Follow the lane past the church, pausing to have a look round if the church is open. Make sure you negotiate the cattle-grid safely and then at the fork in the road, go right, leaving Home Farm on your left. The stretch of water, glimpsed away to the left, is Staunton Harold Reservoir.

Staunton Harold Reservoir and the Calke "Ha Ha"

At the T-junction, now the main exit from the park, go left and follow the lane down past Home Farm to the car park for the reservoir visitors. A permissive path leads straight on, descending to the water's edge. This was the old road before the reservoir flooded the route. A good path now heads to the left, skirting the reservoir. You cross two bridges over feeder streams, then the path swings right to cross over the dam wall. This is not of course the dam for the reservoir itself, but a much older construction, one of a series of dams which formed part of the system of ornamental lakes in Calke Park. Beyond the dam, a flight of steps leads up the "ha-ha" ditch until you reach gates to the left and right. This is the point shown on the map as being a crossing of rights of way, but the routes left and right are firmly barred and gated. Continue up the ha-ha, which soon becomes shallow enough to allow a view to the left over the series of lakes in the Park. Radcliffe power station can be seen away to the right.

At the top of the hill go left alongside the wall, with a deer fence to your left. If you are lucky you may well see some of Calke's red deer herd. At the gate and stile, keep straight on, noting and heeding the warning notice about unfriendly trees throwing branches about. Follow the obvious track until you reach a gate in the wall on the right, just by the electricity pylon. Here you leave the parkland and go back into fields again. Go left alongside the wall, through the gap near the corner, then bear right across the next field, heading for White Leys Farm. Just to the right of the farm there is a stile leading onto a rough lane. On the opposite side of the lane there is another stile which promptly takes you back into fields again.

The map implies that the path is further to the right than it is in practice. Follow the wall on your left, with good views over to the reservoir on your right. Ignore the tempting gateway on the left at the corner of the field and instead, carry on, with the fence cum hedge still to your left. The field boundary bends to the left and a waymarked path goes off to the right, descending quite steeply into the valley bottom. Your route stays alongside the hedge until you reach a gateway on the left. Pass through this and go right, alongside the hedge, until you reach a track just by the wood. Bear left here, following the track as it skirts the southern edge of the wood. There are occasional glimpses of water through the trees, for this area was once a quarry and the old workings are now either flooded or completely overgrown. Either way they are a haven for wildlife.

Return to Tinknall

The track soon turns right and enters the woodland. Follow it closely through the trees, deviating neither to left or right, though there are odd little paths running off here and there. Soon you reach the edge of the trees and pass a few old cottages. The track becomes a rough road and then joins the main A514. Go left here, crossing the main road near the garage to reach the comparative safety of the footway. Note the pump on the left, one of a series in this village. Proceed along the main road, passing under the Ticknall Arch, not a former gateway into the village, but the route of the old tramway, built in 1800 and which served the limestone quarries on the right. Just beyond the arch is the gateway to Calke Park and the start of the two mile long entrance drive. The lodge on the left backed up to the tramway and the embankment is now used as a garden, while still containing the stone block sleepers.

A final quick sprint through the village takes you back to the Wheel again. You have come Full Circle!

29: WESTON UNDERWOOD

The Route: Weston Underwood – Chilla Carr Pit – RAF Memorial –Burlandgreen Lane – Moseyley – Gunhills – Puss in Boots – Windleyhill Farm – Newlands – Woodfall Lane – Draycott Plantation – Weston Underwood

Distance: 5.75 miles (9.25km)

Start: Lay-by near telephone box, on Bullhurst Lane, Weston Underwood. Grid reference: 292426

Map(s): OS 1:25000 Pathfinder Series No. 811, Belper.

How to get there:

By Public Transport: Monday to Saturday bus service from Derby, Ashbourne and Nottingham.

By Car: Follow the signs to Kedleston from Derby, until the left turn is reached just beyond the park. Carry straight on here along the main road and thus reach Weston Underwood about 1.5 miles further on. From A517 take the Muggington road at Cross o' th' Hands and continue on this road to Weston.

The Pub

The Puss in Boots at Windley is a grand unspoiled pub and deservedly popular. It has two rooms, a snug and a lounge, with low beamed ceilings. It was originally the house belonging to the manager of a nearby mill. The mill has long since vanished. It was on the site of the pub car park. Bass Bitter, Ruddles County and Marstons Pedigree are all served on hand-pumps. Opening hours are from 12noon – 3pm and 6pm – 11pm on Mondays to Saturdays, 12noon – 3pm and 7pm – 10.30pm on Sundays. Food is served daily from 12noon – 2pm, and in the evenings.

The Walk

From the telephone box, walk up Bullhurst Lane to its junction with Burlandgreen Lane. Turn left here and go past the houses, one of which boasts an impressive array of aerials, until Pennine House is reached. Go left here, through a waymarked gate and so leave the road.

The Puss in Boots

In the field, bear left by the hedge and follow it down to a footbridge. There is no sign of a path in this field, which sets the pattern for the rest of the walk. Once over the footbridge, bear right and go up the field to reach a stile by the white gate. In the next field, head straight up the middle, towards the second pylon from the right and there, in the hedge, is a waymarked stile. This leads into an area of very high grass and scrub. A machete would be a useful addition to your walking kit at this juncture. Keep the hedge to your right and follow a sketchy path to reach the edge of Chilla Carr Pit. Two waymarks point you in the right direction, along a narrow but distinct track, with the disused and now well vegetated pit on the left. The path is waymarked past the pit and out into the fields again.

More Map Discrepancies

Here the path bears right through a gap in the hedge by the oak tree. The route is then waymarked along the hedge-side, though the map shows a line across the middle of the field. Follow the waymarked route

to the corner of the field and there turn right, to reach a stile in the
hedge on the left by the dead tree. Disconcertingly there is a sign here
saying "Beware of the Bull", though there was nothing remotely resem-
bling a bull when the walk was reconnoitred. Go straight across the
bull's field to a stile in the opposite hedge to the right of the gate.

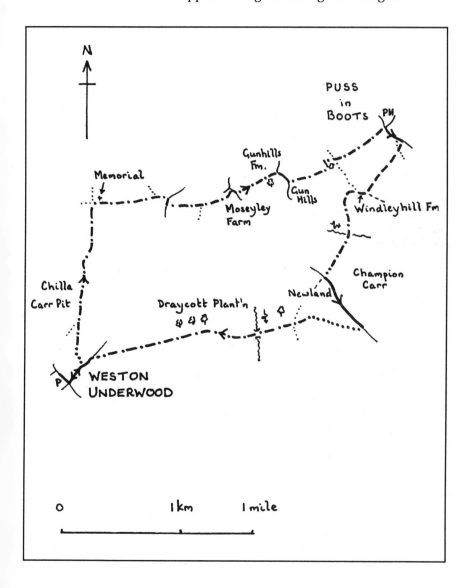

An Isolated Memorial

The map shows a "crossroads" of paths in the middle of this field, but none of the routes are obvious on the ground. Your route lies to the right, past the cross in the middle of the field. This commemorates the crew of an RAF plane which crashed on July 24th 1944. Beyond the cross, go through the gate and then proceed through the next field. Keep the hedge on your left, to reach a waymarked stile near a dew-pond. Continue straight on with the hedge to your left and so reach the brow of the hill. A good view opens up ahead towards Windley and Duffield.

Straight on now, along a good track to a gate which takes you out onto Burlandgreen Lane again. Go right here and then almost at once go left, through a waymarked, but difficult to open, gate. No obvious path presents itself, but keep alongside the hedge on the left. The first boundary reached is easily negotiated as there is a gate-sized gap. Continue straight ahead, still with the hedge on the left to a waymarked gate, which actually opens. The map shows another path joining here, but there's no sign of it in practice. Still with the hedge left, proceed to the next gate, which has neither waymark nor any pretensions to open. Scale this as best you can and land carefully in the muddy approach to Moseylea Farm.

The Passage of Moseylea Farm

Another waymarked gate leads you into the farm complex. The track wriggles left, through the gap between the barns, to reach a gate onto the road again. For the third time of asking this is Burlandgreen Lane. There is a stile almost opposite, but slightly to the left and this is your route. In the field, bear right towards the pole in the middle of the field. Here there is a nettle guarded stile, which has to be negotiated. Keep up the field alongside the hedge, towards the twin poled pylon. Straight on through the jungle of bracken to find another stile. The path then heads up alongside the hedge, towards the left-hand corner of Gunhills Wood. By the standards of these walks, this is quite a steep ascent, but there is a good view from the top, with Alport Hill to the left.

The next stile is well hidden, down a steep bank to the left by an oak tree. In the next field bear left, down the hill towards the corrugated metal hut near Gunhills Farm. The stile is soon spotted. It is by the white post beyond the holly tree. The path now emerges onto Gunhills Lane. Go right here and ascend the lane. At the top of the hill there is a signpost and stile on the left, opposite the ash tree. Leave the road at this point and go into the field. Keep the hedge to your right for a short distance until you reach a stile, then having climbed over this, head across the next field to a stile to the right of the large tree.

A Choice Between Purism and Slurry

Head diagonally left across this next field to a stile in the corner by the post. Straight on towards the big tree, then at the fence corner go right, skirting the slurry lagoon, to reach a waymarked gate. The map shows the right of way passing through the slurry pit, but even the most purist among you will draw the line at that!

The waymarked gate is an important crossing of paths. It is all too easy to stick to the track by the hedge on the right, but this is not your route. Once through the gate, bear left, diagonally down the field to reach a stile in the far corner. Both the corner and the stile are invisible from the gate and it takes quite an act of faith to set off across the field, especially if there are growing crops in it. Having found the stile and dropped into the next field, go immediately right, through the blue gate, then turn left. Follow the hedge down to a stile by a gate and so reach the road, right opposite the Puss in Boots.

The Puss in Boots is not in a village at all, though ostensibly it is part of Windley. Windley means a clearing for pasture, and the whole of this area was once part of the ancient Duffield Forest. It eventually formed part of the Kedleston Estate.

On to Windleyhill Farm

On leaving the pub, go back up to the main road and cross over, turning left towards Duffield. This is a dangerous junction, as the visibility is not good, so do take care. Keep in single file along the road as there is neither footway nor verge. Continue in this death defying act for about 200 metres. The map shows a path heading off to the right just before a farm track is reached, but the path does not exist. Turn right at the farm track instead and follow this through three fields, until it joins another track at a T-junction. Go right here, following the waymark on the tree and thus reach Windleyhill Farm. The track goes through the farm yard, bearing left by the dutch barn to a gate, beyond which are open fields again. Continue on this good track, which soon turns sharp left to reach a three directional waymarker on a stone gatepost in the corner of the field. In the next field the track fades away to nothing, but your route lies straight across the middle of the field, downwards, to a gate and stile in the bottom hedge and fence, by the stream.

Once over the stream, follow the hedge upwards, well to the right of the clump of pines and ignoring tempting gaps. Where the hedge kinks to the right, continue straight on and upwards, across the middle of the field, heading towards the buildings of Newlands. The exit stile is to the left of the two trees and is marked by a square white board. Here you emerge onto a road again. There is a good view back over the Ecclesbourne valley towards Duffield and beyond.

Annoyingly, the tempting track opposite the stile is not a right of way, so you are forced to turn left, along Woodfall Lane, which is fortunately lightly trafficked. Continue along the lane for about 500 metres, then, past the second gate on the right, just where the verge broadens out, there is a stile, which is waymarked. Go through this stile into the field and head diagonally across, to the right of the three trees. On this alignment you should reach the corner of a hedge on your right. Continue alongside this hedge, heading for the pylon. A gate on the right near the pylon leads into a narrow rough lane , which is the one you saw earlier at Newlands. The map indicates that the path keeps out of the lane proper and instead runs alongside in the field. This is not the case in practice, so once in the lane, turn left and follow it until you reach a left turn. Here there is a gate straight ahead and your route lies through this into fields again.

Maps? Who'd Use Them?

The path lies straight on, down the middle of the field, to a stile to the left of a gate. This leads onto a bridge over the stream. No obvious path can be discerned in the next field, nor can the far boundary be seen, but if you head up the middle, towards the three trees, you will find a gate, to the right of the second tree from the left. Go through this gate and continue alongside the hedge towards Draycott Plantation. Despite the map showing the hedge being on your right, it is in fact on your left. When you reach the end of the field, there is a trough and a gate on the left, which you negotiate. Then immediately on the right beyond the gate, there is a stile. An indistinct path heads across the middle of the next field making a bee-line for the left-hand corner of the wood. If your navigation is correct, you should reach a stile, mid way along the hedge. The path now takes up a course parallel to the edge of the wood, heading for a stile between the two trees with the dead tops. The stile exists and is waymarked, but it is well defended by nettles and is difficult to scale. This is not made easier by the presence of a well-hidden ditch!

Having cleared this obstacle you head for the white post across a veritable wilderness of bog and willow herb. The path meanders through this area to a stile just to the right of the post and crosses yet another stream. (There is a bridge). The next field slopes gently upwards and the far boundary cannot be seen. Head up the middle of the field, towards the big tree on the horizon, until you join the fence on the left. Keep alongside the hedge until it kinks sharply to the left and then head just to the left of the curious tree with two lots of branches, one above the other. Here you pick up a good track, which goes through a gate and down onto Burlandgreen Lane again. Be careful as you romp down the track, for there may well be an electric fence stretched across. Could be nasty. On reaching the lane go left and thus reach Weston Underwood.

30: WOOLLEY MOOR

The Route: Woolley Moor – New Napoleon – Smithy Cottage – Milltown –Fallgate – Fall Hill – Ashover (pub) – Far Hill – The Fabrick – Alton –Press – Britton Wood – Coldwell Farm – Broomy Wood – Woodhead Lane –Handley – Boar Farm – Woolley Moor

Distance: 7.6 miles (12.25 km). Allow 6-7 hours including pub stop

Start: Public Car Park just east of the New Napoleon pub. Grid reference: 375610

Map(s): OS 1:25000 Pathfinder Series No. 761, Chesterfield

How to get there:

By Public Transport: A Monday to Saturday bus service from Matlock, Clay Cross and Chesterfield.

By Car: A615 from Matlock to Tansley then B6014 to car park. From A61 at Stretton follow B6014 to car park.

The Pub

The Black Swan at Ashover is an excellent pub, serving Stones, Bass and Theakstons beers on hand pump. Home cooked food is served lunchtimes and evenings, Tuesdays to Sundays, but for the sandwich carrying walker there are seats and tables outside, fronting the main street, so you can sit and watch the world go by. Opening hours are Monday to Sunday 12.00noon –3.00pm, Monday to Saturday 7.00pm – 11.00pm, Sunday 7.00pm – 10.30pm. After a session in this hostelry you'll be prepared to believe in the tales of its ghostly inhabitant, though it might only be the Old Peculiar having an effect.

The Walk

From the car park, go left along the B6014. Take care, as there is neither footway, nor any verge. There is a good view to the left over Ogston reservoir towards the sailing club. Pass the New Napoleon pub on the

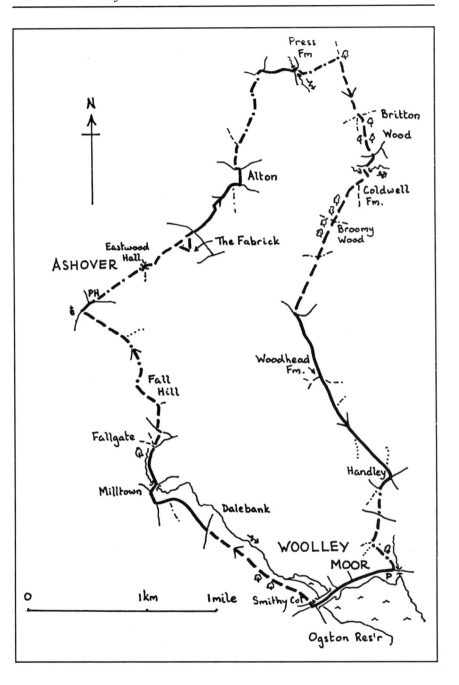

right. This curiously named hostelry is run by Annie Fox and serves John Smiths Ales. There are seats outside and a play area for the children, but it's much too soon to stop if you're going to complete this walk. The pub was originally a private house and was converted to its present use when the Old Napoleon, which was on the opposite side of the road, was demolished during the building of Ogston reservoir in the late 1950s. Most inappropriately, the road leading off to the right is known as Temperance Hill!

Continue along the B6014 past Napoleon Cottage and over the Amber Bridge. The name is that of the river, nothing to do with the colour of the bridge. The bridge spans the river and an arm of the reservoir, usually dry and a haven for wildfowl. The late lamented Ashover Light Railway crossed the road at this point and its course is marked by a spit of higher land running out into the reservoir on your left.

Through the Bluebell Wood

Go up the hill to Smithy Cottage, just beyond the road junction and then go right, over a signposted stile, into the fields. The path is obvious underfoot, running alongside the wall. It passes through another stile and field, to a third stile by a holly tree. There is a good view over Ogston Reservoir from this point. The path now enters a wood, with a steep drop down on the right to the River Amber. The floor of this wood is covered in bluebells in Spring. Another stile takes the path out into open fields again. Keep close to the wall on the left, to pass through another squeezer stile into another field. The Amber is still down on your right, but the scar of the Milltown fluorspar workings is now visible ahead. The village of Woolley Moor is seen perched prominently on the opposite side of the river. Despite local tales of hedgerow wool gathering, the name actually derives from the Old English words meaning Wolves Clearing.

A gate on the left at the far end of the field, leads into a narrow lane and this is followed. At one point the left-hand wall and hedge has vanished, but the route is still obvious. It passes through a further gate with a stile on the right and becomes a muddy lane again. The hedgerows and banks beside the lane have a profusion of wildflowers. Ahead can be seen the frowning bulk of Cocking Tor, fortunately not to be climbed on this walk.

The lane disgorges onto the road at a junction. Carry straight on, along the now tarmac lane, with a view to the right up to the Fabrick Rock on the skyline. As you pass Spencers Cottage on the left, note the curious little clock tower.

At the next T-junction, go right and descend past the Pinfold on the left, to reach the Miners Arms at Milltown. Proud owners of Pub Walks in the Peak District Vol. 1, will recognise this place as one of the hostelries mentioned therein. You are allowed to pop in for old times sake, though it is not the pub featured in this walk.

Over the Ashover Light Railway

Keep to the left of the Miners and take the path between the pub and the cottages, passing the stone trough with its steps, to reach the steel posts marking the site of the former Ashover Light Railway. Ignore the path along the railway alignment. It is neither a right of way, nor does it go where you want. At the next fork in the path, go right and follow a muddy path through the new plantation. The path swings left to follow the river bank. The fluorspar washery at Fallgate is now on your left. Just by a little waterfall, the path briefly emerges into the industrial wasteland, then swings right to cross a bridge. Go over the bridge and then turn left, along the road.

Where the road bears right, there is a wide access drive to the left and a bridleway sign. Do not go this way, but go straight on, leaving the road and seeking out an ivy covered stile to the right of the private driveway. Go through this stile, over the little stone bridge and ascend the narrow path to emerge on the road alongside Greenbank House. Here go left and, almost at once, cross the road and go up the steps to a stile into open fields.

An indistinct path keeps alongside the fence on the left, heading to a stile to the left of the green huts. Heed the warning notice as far as the huts are concerned, but it doesn't apply to the path.

Don't Fall into Fall Hill Quarry!

The path runs to the left of the huts, the remnants of a former fluorspar works. To the left of the path is the deep, water filled pit of a now abandoned fluorspar working. Quite impressive, but dangerous. Don't lean too far over the fence and keep children and dogs on a tight lead.

At the stile by the gate, go left and head uphill to another stile with black metal posts. Here the path enters a little wood, the floor of which is carpeted with dog's mercury. The path winds its way up through the wood, with Fall Hill quarry on the left and heavily overgrown fluorspar workings to the right. Two stiles in quick succession take you out into open fields again. Continue round the left-hand edge of the field to a stile to the right of the metal gate. Go through this and then go right, following the sign, by the wall. Ignore the inviting open gateway and continue along the edge of the field to a stile. From here the ruins of Eastwood Hall can be seen to the right, with the Fabrick crowning the hilltop.

Upon St. Crispin's Day – The Alternative to Shakespeare's Version

The way ahead lies through a series of stiles with the wall first on your right and then on your left, always heading towards the spire of Ashover Church. The path runs along the back of the playing fields as a narrow lane, before emerging in the centre of the village by the Institute, opposite the Crispin Inn and the church. If you have time, look into the church, which has a 15th century spire, though the rest of the building is much earlier. The pub's sign must be one of the largest in the country, telling the tale of the founding of the pub after the Battle of Agincourt in 1417, and going on to describe a Civil War incident in 1646, when the landlord was unceremoniously thrown out of his own pub by drunken Parliamentary troops. Ashover village is blessed with three pubs, all good hostelries. It seems a shame to have to single one out. To the left, beyond the church, lies the Red Lion. The Crispin has already been described. To the right lies the Black Swan, the chosen venue for this walk.

As you emerge from the Black Swan, go left, along the road for a short distance, then left again, through a kissing gate, by the side of a private drive. The path is signposted. The path is not distinct in the field, but keeps to the left of the clump of trees, which fringes the swallet hole. Streams emerge from the sides of the hole then disappear down the centre, a sure sign that you are in limestone country. Ashover has all the geological features of Derbyshire, but in miniature, the limestone, the gritstone edges, coal measures and shales.

Chance to Kiss and Make Up

Beyond the clump of trees, the path makes a bee-line for the Fabrick and soon passes through another kissing gate to run alongside a rail fence. At the next kissing gate – a fine path this for lovers – the path forks. The left-hand route is private and leads up to the drive to Eastwood Grange, now a conference centre. The right-hand way, which is your route, goes under the drive by a bridge and begins to climb quite steeply. You soon pass under a second bridge and then climb a short flight of steps to reach a lane. Go left here, then almost at once bear right at the metal gate, leaving the lane and entering fields again.

Continue steeply up, with the wall on your right, passing through a stile and into another field. Look out now for a stile in the wall on your right. It is waymarked. Go through this stile and leave the cultivated fields behind for the rough moor of the Fabrick. Climb left up the slope, using the rough hewn steps provided. At the crest of the hill, go right to reach the Fabrick itself. Look out for the carved figure of a donkey and the letters TSSF on the stones to the right.

The Fabrick Rock

The View from The Fabrick

The view from the summit is magnificent, with Ashover far below. There is a viewing platform a little further on, but it is unfortunately positioned slightly wrong, so the indicated sights are not in the places they should be. Nevertheless, you can see four counties from this point and if it is a fine clear day, it is worth lingering to admire the view.

Leave the Fabrick by one of the many paths heading north east i.e. away from Ashover and towards the road. At the road, go to the junction and follow the lane signed to Alton. At the 'S' bend there is the fine red brick hall, and then Alton village is reached. The road swings right to a T-junction. Here go left and so reach a triangular junction. There is a telephone box at the triangle which looks as if only a midget could get inside, but it is an illusion caused by a difference in levels of the three roads. At the triangle, bear left and cross the road onto a rough track, past Townfield House. The track continues past the delightfully named Candlelight Cottages and then, just alongside the old quarry on the left, there is a gate and stile on the right.

Go over the stile and descend the narrow, muddy field to a gate on the left-hand side. Go through this gate into an L-shaped field. The path bears right and cuts across the field to a stile half way along the wall, on the right of the second hawthorn. There is quite a drop from this stile into the next field. The path then cuts left across this field, to a stile in the left-hand wall, above two more thorn trees. Annoyingly this takes you back into the L-shaped field you left a few moments ago! The path now runs across the field, keeping close to the wall, to reach a stile in the far corner. In the next field the path follows the wall again to reach a gateway on the right. Here go right and descend towards the clump of larches.

At the larches, go left and descend to the lane. Go right here, bearing right again at the road junction, following the signs for Clay Cross. At the T-junction, go left, along the lane signed to Wingerworth, and descend to the bridge across the Press Brook. Just before the bridge, there is a path to the right, unsigned and easily missed. This leads alongside the stream to a stone clapper bridge. Once over the bridge, the path wriggles its way through the bushes and scrub to a stile, which gives out into fields again. Keep left by the hedge, through a couple more fields, each with a stile in place, and ascend gently towards a clump of trees on the horizon. The path is muddy in places, but your attention will be more focussed on the seemingly impenetrable holly hedge at the far end of the field, right where the stile should be. Luckily, the obstacle proves to be a sham. There is a perfectly easy stile found just to the left of the holly. This leads out onto another path, where you turn right.

There used to be quarry workings here, though they are long disused and heavily overgrown. The resultant trees, bushes, hummocks and hollows, make this a good spot for a picnic. To the left lies Bole Hill, one of the many such names on this eastern fringe of Derbyshire and all indicative of ancient smelting sites.

Britton Wood

The path now follows the hedge down through a stile into fields, where good views open up eastwards towards Clay Cross. Still keeping close to the hedge on the right, the path passes through another field, to reach a gap in the fence surrounding Britton Wood. Go into the scrub which fringes the wood and bear left, ignoring the path going straight on. Descend until you reach a "crossroads" of paths and here go straight ahead into the wood proper. Britton Wood is a delightful mixture of tree types, without the usual gloom of conifer plantations. The path is followed without difficulty, down through the wood to a muddy gateway and so out onto the road.

Go to the road junction and turn right by the "mobile" homes, then go left, down the lane signed to Coldwell Farm. This lane dips to cross Press Brook, then rises steeply in a zig-zag, over the cattle-grid, to reach the farm buildings.

The map shows a path to the right of the farm buildings, but a painted sign directs you left, along the track, to pass between two cattle sheds, one of which has been built on the line of the mapped path. On reaching the main farm house, another painted sign advises a route straight ahead and another to the right, through a gate, into the farmyard. Your route is the one to the right. Go through the gate into the farmyard and bear right to reach another gate between two barns. The route is marked again with painted signs. The right of way now goes through this next gate, skirts the left-hand barn and then turns left up the hill, through the inevitable collection of old farm machinery. Beyond the machinery there is a gate and stile and thus the path reaches open fields again.

I Spy Roman Legions

he track proceeds through a series of fields, always with the wall or edge on the right and sticking to the top of the ridge. The view west is ocked by Broomy Wood, but eastwards the vista is extensive. Particu-rly prominent is Stretton, perched on the ridge carrying the main A61 ad, once the Roman Ryknield Street.

e path leaves Broomy Wood behind and the view west opens up to lude Alton and Littlemoor. Ignore paths crossing the ridge and ntinue along the hilltop to a gate with a well hidden stile. This brings u out onto a lane, opposite a road junction. Go across the road and wn Woodhead Lane, which is signed to Handley. Again this has very good views eastward, but the view to the west is restricted because the lane is slightly below the ridge top. Continue along this lightly trafficked lane for about a mile, passing Woodhead Farm about a third of the way along. The lane is narrow but there are the remains of causeway stones on the right-hand side in places.

Handley is soon reached at a cross roads, where there is a seat on the right. Go right, over the brow of the hill and, at the footpath sign by the bend, leave the road and go left into the fields.

The End in Sight

The path in these fields is scarcely visible, but runs diagonally across, cutting below the prominent holly bushes, to a stile in the far corner. Ogston Reservoir is now in view ahead. Negotiate the stile, which has seen better days and go right, to another stile a short distance ahead that gives out onto the B6036. Cross the road with care and go straight on down the farm track towards the solitary tree and to the left of the farmhouse. Where the track turns right into the farmyard, make your way over a very wet patch and go through a stile in the hedge straight in front.

Head left now, following the hedge and fence and noting that the OS map suggests that this path should be on the opposite side of the fence. Don't worry, you're right, the map wrong. Carry on along the fence to a tumbledown wall ahead, with a rough semblance of a stile in it. Scramble over this obstacle and continue alongside the hedge in the next field, with Ogston in view ahead. Don't stray too far from the hedge or you will miss the exit stile and spend an exasperating ten minutes hunting for a way out of the field. The hedge has a slight right and left kink and the stile is at this point, well to the left of the house.

Once over the stile, the path is in woodland and descends sketchily t the stream, through the carpet of wild garlic. No sooner does it reach th brook than it scrambles away again, climbing up to the right to a stil onto the B6014, directly opposite the car park.

We publish guides to individual towns, plus books on walking and cycling in the great outdoors throughout England and Wales. This is a recent selection:

Local Guidebooks

OLD NOTTINGHAMSHIRE REMEMBERED – Keith Taylor *(£7.95)*

STRANGE SOUTH YORKSHIRE – David Clarke *(£6.95)*

CHESHIRE: its magic and mystery – Doug Pickford *(£6.95)*

STAFFORDSHIRE: its magic and mystery – Doug Pickford *(£6.95)*

PORTRAIT OF MACCLESFIELD – Doug Pickford *(£6.95)*

PORTRAIT OF MANCHESTER – John Creighton *(£6.95)*

PORTRAIT OF STOCKPORT – John Creighton *(£6.95)*

PORTRAIT OF WARRINGTON – Jen Darling *(£6.95)*

MACCLESFIELD: THOSE WERE THE DAYS – Doug Pickford *(£7.95)*

MAGIC, MYTH AND MEMORIES: The Peak District – Doug Pickford *(£7.95)*

SUPERNATURAL STOCKPORT – Martin Mills *(£5.95)*

SHADOWS: a northern investigation of the unknown – Steve Cliffe *(£7.95)*

Country Walking . . .

RAMBLES AROUND NOTTINGHAM & DERBY – Keith Taylor *(£6.95)*

SECRET YORK: WALKS WITHIN THE CITY WALLS – Les Pierce *(£6.95)*

FIFTY CLASSIC WALKS IN THE PENNINES – Terry Marsh *(£8.95)*

WALKING PEAKLAND TRACKWAYS – Mike Cresswell *(£7.95)*

MOSTLY DOWNHILL IN THE PEAK DISTRICT – Clive Price
(two volumes: White Peak & Dark Peak, £6.95 each)

EAST CHESHIRE WALKS – Graham Beech *(£5.95)*

WEST CHESHIRE WALKS – Jen Darling *(£5.95)*

WEST PENNINE WALKS – Mike Cresswell *(£5.95)*

RAMBLES AROUND MANCHESTER – Mike Cresswell *(£5.95)*

⌐H WALKS: Dolgellau /Cambrian Coast: L. Main & M. Perrott *(£5.95)*

WELSH WALKS: Aberystwyth & District – L. Main & M. Perrott *(£5.95)*

Cycling...

CYCLE UK! The essential guide to leisure cycling – Les Lumsdon *(£9.95)*

OFF-BEAT CYCLING IN THE PEAK DISTRICT – Clive Smith *(£6.95)*

MORE OFF-BEAT CYCLING IN THE PEAK DISTRICT – Clive Smith *(£6.95)*

50 BEST CYCLE RIDES IN CHESHIRE – edited by Graham Beech *(£7.95)*

CYCLING IN THE COTSWOLDS – Stephen Hill *(£6.95)*

CYCLING IN THE CHILTERNS – Henry Tindell *(£7.95)*

CYCLING IN SOUTH WALES – Rosemary Evans *(£7.95)*

CYCLING IN LINCOLNSHIRE – Penny & Bill Howe *(£7.95)*

CYCLING IN STAFFORDSHIRE – Linda Wain *(£7.95)*

CYCLING IN THE LAKE DISTRICT – John Wood *(£7.95)*

Explore the Lake District with Sigma!

THE LAKELAND SUMMITS: a survey of the fells of the Lake District National Park – Tim Synge *(£7.95)*

LAKELAND ROCKY RAMBLES: Geology beneath your feet – Brian Lynas *(£9.95)*

100 LAKE DISTRICT HILL WALKS – Gordon Brown *(£7.95)*

PUB WALKS IN THE LAKE DISTRICT – Neil Coates *(£6.95)*

FULL DAYS ON THE LAKELAND FELLS – Adrian Dixon *(£7.95)*

TEASHOP WALKS IN THE LAKE DISTRICT – Jean Patefield *(£6.95)*

LAKELAND WALKING, ON THE LEVEL – Norman Buckley *(£6.95)*

MOSTLY DOWNHILL: LEISURELY WALKS, LAKE DISTRICT – Alan Pears *(£6.95)*

STROLLING WITH STEAM: walks along the Keswick railway – Jan Darrall *(£4.9.)*

Pub Walks...

A fabulous series of 'Pub Walks' books for just about every popular walking area in UK, all featuring access by public transport

– plus many more entertaining and educational books being regularly adde
our list. All of our books are available from your local bookshop. In case
difficulty, or to obtain our complete catalogue, please contact:

Sigma Leisure, 1 South Oak Lane, Wilmslow, Cheshire SK9 6A
Phone: 0625 – 531035   Fax: 0625 – 536800

ACCESS and VISA orders welcome – call our friendly sales staff or us
24 hour Answerphone service! Most orders are despatched on the d
receive your order – you could be enjoying our books in just a couple o

NOTES